MW00559361

ADVANCE PRAISE

"Debbie Zacarian and Ivannia Soto masterfully translate culturally responsive and sustaining pedagogy into practical, ready-to-implement strategies for teachers of culturally and linguistically diverse students. Their new book is a much-needed resource that will help all educators create empowering learning environments and apply effective instructional practices that build on students' strengths rather than focus on deficiencies!"

—**Andrea Honigsfeld,** Author and Professor, Molloy College

"Debbie Zacarian and Ivannia Soto's *Responsive Schooling for Culturally and Linguistically Diverse Students* is a timely new contribution to the conversation around supporting CLD students. Zacarian and Soto present a rare combination of relevant research, theory, and opportunities for real-world application, drawing from their vast expertise in the field. I highly recommend this book for all teachers to ensure they have the latest tools at their fingertips to provide CLD students a more equitable education."

—**Diane Staehr Fenner, Ph.D.,** President, SupportEd, LLC

"The authors address valuable questions the field is asking: Why culturally responsive teaching, and what does this look like? They demonstrate a balanced approach to instruction and provide ways in which schools can work with parents and community. Additionally, the scenarios, tips, reflection tasks, and other tools give the reader opportunities to discuss in learning communities how to adapt and implement these great ideas."

—**Margarita Calderón, Ph.D.,** Professor Emerita, Johns Hopkins University

"*Responsive Schooling* exemplifies today's educational movement toward enhanced inclusion and empowerment of multilingual learners and their families. With emphasis on enriching opportunities and equity in schools, Zacarian and Soto illustrate the assets and contributions of this growing student population to create linguistically and culturally sustainable classrooms. This go-to resource helps educators better understand the importance of building student identity and partnerships through strategies of engagement and co-construction to shape a collaborative, socially responsive learning environment."

—**Margo Gottlieb, Ph.D.,** WIDA Co-founder and Lead Developer, University of Wisconsin–Madison

NORTON BOOKS IN EDUCATION

Responsive Schooling
for Culturally and Linguistically
Diverse Students

Responsive Schooling
for Culturally and Linguistically
Diverse Students

DEBBIE ZACARIAN AND IVANNIA SOTO

W. W. NORTON & COMPANY
Independent Publishers Since 1923

Note to Readers: This work is intended as a general information resource for teachers, administrators and others who work with students who are culturally and linguistically diverse and their caregivers. Although the authors have extensive experience in the subject matter, neither they nor the publisher can guarantee that any educational approach, strategy or technique that this book describes or proposes will work with every individual student, parent, or caregiver. None of the authors is a lawyer, and nothing stated in this book should be construed as legal advice.

Names and potentially identifying characteristics of individual students and educators other than the authors have been changed. Any URLs displayed in this book link or refer to websites that existed as of press time. The publisher is not responsible for, and should not be deemed to endorse or recommend, any website other than its own or any content, including any app, that it did not create. The authors, also, are not responsible for any third-party material.

Library of Congress Cataloging-in-Publication Data

Names: Zacarian, Debbie, author. | Soto, Ivannia, author.
Title: Responsive schooling for culturally and linguistically diverse students / Debbie
    Zacarian and Ivannia Soto.
Description: First edition. | New York : W.W. Norton & Company, 2020. |
Series: Norton books in education | Includes bibliographical references and index.
Identifiers: LCCN 2019047645 | ISBN 9780393713527 (paperback) |
    ISBN 9780393713534 (epub)
Subjects: LCSH: Culturally relevant pedagogy—United States. | Minorities—
    Education—United States. | Limited English-proficient students—United States. |
    Community and school—United States.
Classification: LCC LC1099.515.C85 Z34 2020 | DDC 370.117—dc23
LC record available at https://lccn.loc.gov/2019047645

W. W. Norton & Company, Inc., 500 Fifth Avenue, New York, N.Y. 10110
www.wwnorton.com

W. W. Norton & Company Ltd., 15 Carlisle Street, London W1D 3BS

1 2 3 4 5 6 7 8 9 0

Contents

Acknowledgments

We express our gratitude to several people who contributed to this book. At Norton, Carol Collins supported us throughout the genesis and drafting process, and Mariah Eppes and Jamie Vincent throughout the editing and production process. A very special thanks goes to our spouses for their support throughout the writing project.

We dedicate this book to students, families, and scholars. They show us how we can work and learn together to create responsive and sustaining classrooms for diverse learners, and there is no better time to do just that than right now.

Introduction

IN THERESA LAFONTAINE's second-grade class, students are studying how to multiply single-digit numbers. For homework, they were given five word problems to complete from the course text. The first problem asks students to calculate how much orange juice can be made from one cup of orange juice concentrate by adding three cups of water. Here is an exchange that Mrs. LaFontaine has with Janeen, a student in her class.

MRS. LAFONTAINE: Janeen, let's look at your homework assignment.

JANEEN: It be at home.

MRS. LAFONTAINE: Hmmm. Okay, let's talk about the problems. Were you able to complete them?

JANEEN: It be hard. I don' get the book (She says with her eyes facing the floor).

MRS. LAFONTAINE: What was hard?

JANEEN: What be concentrate? (She asks quietly).

MRS. LAFONTAINE: Concentrate?

JANEEN: Yea, juice concentrate?

MRS. FONTAINE: Oh! I see. Did you know that there are different meanings for that word, concentrate?

JANEEN: What?

MRS. LAFONTAINE: Yes! Concentrate is what we do in school and at home and everywhere when we focus our brains on something. So, that is like an action that we take, we concentrate. Right?

JANEEN: Yes.

MRS. LAFONTAINE: Well, the very same word, concentrate, is also a thing or what we call a noun. It is used to describe one of the ways people make things like juice drinks. It's when they take lots of orange juice and then remove most of the water from it and put what is left in a can. What's in the can is then called concentrate. It's like all of the contents of the juice without the water. And, when we put the water back in, it makes it orange juice again.

JANEEN: Wow, dat's weird (She says with her eyes opened wide).

MRS. LAFONTAINE: Let's see if we can find a video of it so you can see how it works. If we can't, I will try to bring some in, okay?

JANEEN: Okay.

MRS. LAFONTAINE: So, let's say that you have one cup of water and you want to make three times as much. How many cups would you have?

Many of us have witnessed exchanges like this one or had them ourselves at home or in our workplace. It is almost impossible not to notice the different ways that we all communicate, especially as our schools become more and more culturally and linguistically diverse. Mrs. LaFontaine and Janeen's interaction is an example of the everyday conversations that are occurring around us.

In our book, we present a variety of reflection tasks, such as the following one. Our intent is for readers to stop, reflect, and respond to the idea or concept that we have discussed by responding to the reflection task that we ask. With this in mind, complete the following reflection task.

As you read the exchange between Mrs. LaFontaine and Janeen, what did you notice? _____

_____

_____

_____

_____

_____

We have asked many educators this question. Some respond that the student, Janeen, is quite open with her teacher about what she finds challenging. They often elaborate saying that she could specifically recall a question from the course text and describe the difficulties that she had in understanding one of the terms. Others tell us that they are troubled by what they perceive is her lack of "standard" English or school language. Some also extend that thought by telling us that Mrs. LaFontaine has to do much more than teach Janeen basic mathematics. At a professional development session on culturally responsive teaching, several teachers lamented the amount of precious time that Mrs. LaFontaine had to "take away" from the mathematics lesson "just to help her student learn how we use language in school."

Perhaps you found yourself responding to our question with a variant of the various responses that we have heard. Perhaps, you also found yourself using evaluative language that ranged from *how well* the student was able to identify the challenge that she had in completing the problem to *how poorly* the student uses language. These opposing points of view reflect where we are in education. Some of us struggle endlessly securing the just-right "cure" for what we believe is wrong with students such as Janeen by using a model of instruction that reflects our desire, and even pressure from outside forces, to remedy what we believe are deficits. Some of us focus almost solely on what students such as Janeen are doing well because we believe so strongly in seeing what's there and not what's missing.

Our book looks at the type of classroom discourse that is needed for culturally responsive and sustained classroom conversations, tasks, and activities where everyone is empowered because they feel a sense of belonging and being safe, valued, acknowledged, competent, and socially responsive to the needs and interests of their peers and of society itself. Many educational scholars and practitioners use the terms *culturally responsive* and *culturally sustaining* interchangeably, and we do as well. We define the core of culturally responsive and culturally sustaining approaches as being akin to the steps that our field has taken for teachers to:

- move away from being the all-knowing authority where classroom communication is controlled by and flows through the teacher;
- move toward engaging every classroom member in a co-constructed and collaborative approach in which all are empowered and have a voice; and
- draw from the diverse personal, social, cultural, and linguistic assets of students by using a strengths-based approach.

The type of empowered, culturally responsive, sustaining learning environment that we promote in our book calls for educators to embrace, in our deeds and actions, the rapidly changing and diverse student and family populations that are entering our schools by acknowledging the strengths of what students are communicating as opposed to what we perceive as missing in the learning or even the lives of students. An example of what we mean are the perceptions that occurred during the aftermath of the hurricanes that devastated Puerto Rico, the U.S. Virgin Islands, and portions of Houston and Miami. Thousands of students moved with and without their parents to communities that represented cultures, languages, climates, and other characteristics that were quite distinct from their home communities. Many educators perceived such students as having deficits (such as "they don't speak English") and so sympathetically (such as "those poor students lost everything") that it was hard for them to see the many strengths that the same students and families possessed *and* enacted as a demonstration of their remarkable resilience. Examples such as these, and countless others, require that we urgently begin looking beyond the surface of *what* we teach and *who* we perceive that we teach to how we can be more responsive and embracing to truly meet the dynamic changes that are occurring in our student and family populations.

Our book looks closely at the big picture of what is occurring in *what* we teach (e.g., our approaches to content and curriculum instruction) to best ensure that it matches the *who* we are teaching in terms of our students' dynamically changing identities. We also examine how we can look productively at the moment-to-moment interactions/conversations that we have with students, they have with each other, we have about them, and so forth, so that we are proactive in using practices that continuously reinforce a reciprocal disposition of mutual respect, value, and competence. The following describes each of the chapters in our book.

Chapter 1: What's the Urgency for Culturally Responsive Teaching in Contemporary Education? This chapter will present the urgency for redefining academic language learning as a culturally responsive practice that involves a balanced, mutually respectful approach to school *and* home language(s) as well as students' and families' cultural ways of being. We explore the urgent need to re-examine the imbalanced weight toward educators' relentless pursuit of academic language. We describe this as an equity issue and discuss the historic roots of this pursuit. We also include a summary of key court cases and initiatives that were intended to remedy inequities. We will explain that while each of these included actions were intended to close the opportunity gap among dominant and underrepresented populations, they also served to further privilege one group of students—those who already possess academic language and American middle-class expectations about schooling—and, in doing so, resulted in maintaining or widening the opportunity gap among various groups of students. Further, we will discuss how the overemphasis on academic language and away from home and community cultures has weakened, in varying degrees of intensity, languages, cultures, and practices other than academic language and dominant middle-class U.S. cultural practices and has caused the devaluation and even the loss of these culturally responsive practices. We will present a discussion of some of the asset-based models, which emphasize the strengths of the various cultures and languages of students to show how these models affirm, acknowledge, and, particularly, emphasize the various competencies of students' sociocultural and linguistic strengths.

Chapter 2: Understanding Identity as Socially and Interactionally Constructed. In this chapter, we define cultural identity as expressed through the language that we use to communicate, in various contexts, as well as our identities and ways of being and acting. We describe child development as involving repeated and continuous interactions that a child observes or engages with or among their parents/guardians, family, family community, school community, and the local community in which the child is reared. We will discuss how each of these interactional events reflects the rich interactions that comprehensively help in supporting each child's development of their personal, cultural, and social worldview and identity.

Chapter 3: Building a Balanced Approach to Culturally Responsive Teaching. In this chapter, we will articulate a culturally responsive approach to education where the "what" and "who" we teach involves a matched, balanced approach where students' personal, cultural, and social identities are central to the curriculum that is chosen, and the approaches that are used to teach are meaningfully and socially connected around issues of social justice and equity. We will include a detailed discussion about collective versus independent cultural views drawing from Geert Hofstede and others. The chapter will include classroom scenarios that demonstrate independent and collectivist cultural practices in the classroom setting and structures that need to be in place for culturally responsive classrooms.

Chapter 4: Building Culturally Responsive Family–School Partnerships. In this chapter, we will discuss the importance of family-school engagement and show approaches and authentic examples of culturally responsive practices that connect students' home and community experiences to the classroom. The chapter will include an extension of our interactive framework and examples of promising practices and models to contextualize the principles presented in the chapter.

Chapter 5: Building Culturally Responsive Schools. In this chapter, we will move beyond the classroom to the school to describe approaches and authentic examples of culturally responsive school-wide practices. The chapter will include an extension of our interactive framework and examples of promising practices and models to contextualize the principles presented in the chapter.

Chapter 6: Building Culturally Responsive School–Community Connections. In this chapter, we will move beyond the school to the community to create active school-community partnerships that the school/district community built and active partnerships with local community members, agencies, civic and business organizations that are built from our culturally responsive framework. The chapter will include an extension of our interactive framework and examples of promising practices to contextualize the principles presented in the chapter.

Chapter 7: Service-learning as a Culturally Responsive Practice. This chapter will focus on the key principles and approaches for students to contribute to their school and local communities through service-learning projects in which they address issues that are relevant to the school/district communities in which they learn and local communities in which they live. In this chapter, we will describe the steps needed for creating meaningful culturally responsive service-learning projects within a school/district as a means to cement and infuse the principles presented in our book. We will also include steps for service-learning that involve securing and partnering with culturally responsive businesses and community-based agencies and partners: The Framingham Public Schools in Framingham, MA where multiple internship opportunities are provided to students enrolled in the dual language programs during their senior year, and the Brockton Public Schools in Brockton, MA who provides a medical interpretation program of study in multiple languages. We will also draw from the following to illustrate service-learning projects in practice: a freshman writing course at Whittier College with the theme, "Identity Formation," where college students engage in unpacking culturally responsive texts around race/ethnicity, gender, and religion and also conduct a service-learning project with ELLs at Whittier High School (WHS). The course requires that students write two essays based on their contextualized, culturally responsive experiences at WHS.

In our first chapter, we begin our conversation about culturally responsive teaching by drawing from the example we presented at the opening of this introduction to frame what we mean as culturally responsive teaching as it applies to our dynamically changing student and family populations.

Responsive Schooling for Culturally and Linguistically Diverse Students

1

What's the Urgency
for Culturally Responsive Teaching
in Contemporary Education?

IN THE OPENING OF OUR BOOK, we shared an interaction that a teacher had with her student about the homework task she'd been assigned. One of the student's responses was "It be at home." The student's response about the location of her assignment signified her as being what many refer to as a "non-standard" speaker of English (Labov, 2006). The descriptor "non-standard" signifies a difference in what a student says or writes and how we want or expect them to communicate in school settings. For many years, these differences have been described as "variant forms of communication" and even deviant from the expected standard. Descriptors such as these have led many to assume that a student, parent, or other person who uses these variant forms somehow knows less or possesses less language than others. Further, it has also led to the assumption that variants such as these signal a deficit that needs remedying without acknowledging the rich language that is being spoken using forms such as these.

As educators, no matter how strong our commitment and dedication are to our students, we cannot deny the need for strengthening what we do. We begin our discussion about this topic by viewing it from a historic, demographic, and theoretical lens to frame what we mean as culturally responsive teaching. We start by going back in history to 1950.

WHAT IS THE URGENCY FOR USING A CULTURALLY RESPONSIVE APPROACH?

A Historical Perspective

Patricia is a Black student living in Prince Edward County, Virginia in 1950. She has been attending an all-Black school in her community following the 1896 post-Civil War U.S. Supreme Court decision in *Plessy v. Ferguson* that "separate but equal" conditions were constitutional. Her school is far from adequate, or even close to being equal to the school that the White children in her community attend. Her experience as well as thousands of others led to the U.S. Supreme Court's 1954 decision in *Brown v. Board of Education*, which overturned *Plessy v. Ferguson* and mandated that each state desegregate its schools.

However, the decision didn't result in equitable or desperately needed changes in societal practices. The evils of racism continued to plague the country and included the infamous murder of civil rights activists Medgar Evers and William Moore and the deaths of four girls at the 16th Street Baptist Church in 1963. As a result of these and other violent events, President Kennedy began to advocate for legislation that would recognize the civil rights of all of the nation's citizens. Though Kennedy was assassinated in November of that year, his successor, President Johnson, Congress enacted the Civil Rights Act of 1964, which outlawed discrimination on the "basis of race, color, religion, sex, or national origin." During the same year, President Johnson declared a "War on Poverty" advocating for, among other initiatives, the right of all students to receive the same access to a quality public education as everyone in the country.

Section 402 of the Civil Rights Act required that, within two years, the commissioner of education conduct a survey and report to the President and Congress "concerning the lack of availability of equal educational opportunities for individuals by reason of race, color, religion, or national origin in public educational institutions" (EEOC [n.d.]). The study that was conducted to meet this mandate was titled Equality of Educational Opportunity and was known as the *Coleman Report* (Coleman, 1966). It highlighted the inequalities and discriminatory practices that were occurring nationwide, the opportunity gaps that had chronically affected students from underrepresented populations, and the urgency to provide students all students with equal access to an education (Gamoran & Long, 2006). To help close those gaps, in 1965, President Johnson signed the Elementary and Secondary Education Act ("ESEA"). ESEA authorized federal funds for professional development, instructional materials, resources to support educational programs, and the promotion of parental involvement in the schools. Since that time, there have been many developments, including additional court decisions, that have aimed at improving

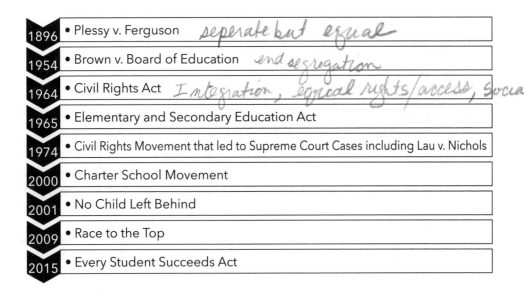

1896	• Plessy v. Ferguson *seperate but equal*
1954	• Brown v. Board of Education *end segregation*
1964	• Civil Rights Act *Integration, equal rights/access, social justice*
1965	• Elementary and Secondary Education Act
1974	• Civil Rights Movement that led to Supreme Court Cases including Lau v. Nichols
2000	• Charter School Movement
2001	• No Child Left Behind
2009	• Race to the Top
2015	• Every Student Succeeds Act

Figure 1.1: Historic Timeline of Key Court Cases and Federal Regulations and Initiatives

the outcomes of underrepresented groups including students of color, students with disabilities, students learning English as an additional language, and students' living in poverty. An example of these is the U.S. Supreme Court ruling in *Lau v. Nichols* that schools must provide programming and services to help students overcome language barriers to learning (Endo and Wong, 2018). All of these initiatives and rulings occurred in large part because of the urgency to end the pervasive practices of discrimination that were occurring. They were also the precursors to later efforts such as the "Charter School Movement" under U.S. President Clinton in 2000, the "No Child Left Behind Act" under U.S. President Bush in 2001, as well as the "Race to the Top" initiative in 2009 and "Every Student Succeeds Act" in 2015 under President Obama (Zacarian, 2011, 2015). Figure 1.1 illustrates the various court cases, initiatives, and actions.

Similarly, Lindsey, Robins, Terrell, and Lindsey (2018) in their work on cultural proficiency, present a timeline for how each decade has created new social policies in response to the current issues of concern with equity work. Their timeline highlights major movements in education and society as follows:

- Prior to the 1950s: Segregation—the legal separation of cultural and racial groups in the United States.
- 1950s: Desegregation—*Brown v. Board of Education* in 1954 ends segregation in public facilities and leads to many legal initiatives.

social policies

- 1960s: Integration, equal access, equal rights—a decade of domestic revolutions; period of activism for social justice and civil rights.
- 1970s: Equal benefits, multiculturalism—people of color strive to extend the legal gains won during the previous decade; multiculturalism a departure from the assimilationist or melting pot model.
- 1980s: Diversity—corporate American begins to support and address diversity-related issues and provide diversity training for employees; aspects of diversity grew to include ethnicity, language, gender, sexual orientation, disability, and age.
- 1990s: Cultural competence—the essential elements of cultural competence provide basic behavior standards for interacting effectively with people who differ from one another.
- 2000s: Cultural proficiency—a way of being that enables people to engage successfully in new environments.

Take a few moments to complete the following two reflection activities.

1. Drawing from the historical perspective that we provided, describe the evidence that you have seen or observed of any of these laws enacted in your particular context.

_____

_____

_____

2. Drawing from your response, what do you believe would occur if these laws were not in place? What might it look like in the context that you described in your response to the first question?

_____

_____

_____

A Demographic Perspective

While many might feel that laws, regulations, and federal actions should have automatically resulted in compliance, the disparities that continue to occur among some groups of underrepresented students tell us a much different story. An example of these disparities is seen in the graduation rates among different groups of students as described in Figure 1.2.

An additional lens through which to view these disparities is the lack of racial and economic diversity of teachers and administrators against the backdrop of rapid demographic shifts in our student and family populations. Consider the following realities:

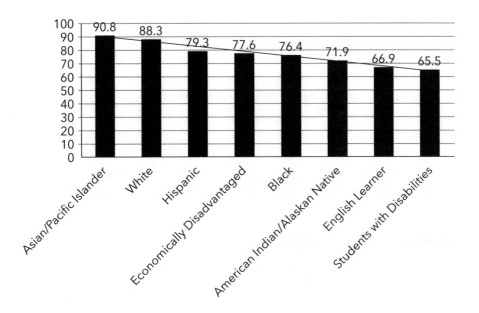

Figure 1.2: U.S. Public School Student Graduation Rates, 2015–2016 *(National Center for Education Statistics [May 2018])*

- Most of the nation's teachers and administrators are White (U.S. Department of Education, 2016) or White and middle class (Hollins & Guzman, 2005).
- Most teacher preparation programs in institutions of higher education are taught by full-time faculty who are White (National Center for Education Statistics, 2018).
- Many teachers who were "fast-tracked" into teaching in poor urban and rural areas were not given adequate training (Zeichner, 2012).
- Suburban schools are rapidly becoming more culturally, economically, linguistically, and racially diverse (Edwards, Domke, & White, 2017).
- More than half the nation's students live in poverty (Southern Education Foundation, 2015).
- English learners (ELs) are one of the most rapidly growing groups in the nation (National Center for Education Statistics, 2018).
- More than half of the nation's students have had one or more significantly adverse childhood experiences (ACEs), including physical, sexual, or verbal abuse; physical or emotional neglect; a parent who is addicted to alcohol or drugs; witnessing a mother who is abused; a family member in jail; the loss of a parent to death, abandonment, or divorce; and/or mental illness of a family member (Data Resource Center for Child and Adolescent Health, 2011/2012).

- While English learners and bilingual bicultural children experience the same adversities as their peers, many are also refugees who have come to the U.S. fleeing crises in their homelands (U.S. Department of State, 2015) and/or are undocumented and citizen children of at least one undocumented parent who live in chronic fear of being deported (Menjívar & Cervantes, 2016).
- Society's definition of what constitutes a family is evolving to include children being raised by two parents, a single parent, a foster parent, a grandparent, blended parents, and/or with extra-familial supports (Zacarian & Silverstone, 2015) as well as those being reared in institutional settings such as undocumented children taken from their parents at the U.S. border (Zacarian & Dove, 2019).

Take a few moments to complete the following reflection activities.

1. Drawing from the demographic realities we provided, describe evidence of these that you have seen or experienced.

   Blended households

2. Drawing from your response to the prior question, what do you believe should occur to best prepare for our changing student populations?

A Research-based Sociocultural and Sociolinguistic Perspective

Since the 1960s, there has been a good deal of research (including by us) on how to work more successfully with students whose culturally, linguistically, and economically diverse experiences are distinct from their educators so that they may flourish in school and in their lives. As we will show, the research calls for educators to use a principled, balanced, and mutually reciprocal and respectful approach to school *and* home language(s).

A helpful place to begin discussing the type of approach that we advocate is the foundational contributions of developmental psychologist Lev Vygotsky (1978). Vygotsky claimed that children learn mainly through social interactions and that children's culture affects what they learn. Indeed, Vygotsky put forth the idea that learning is highly connected to a child's sociocultural context and, as they grow to school age, a student's sociocultural context. Further, he asserted that the relationships among sociocultural relevance, thinking, and learning cannot be underscored enough. It leads to our thinking that we must use culturally responsive practices that:

1. engage students in social interactions that are situated in a familiar cultural context and
2. communicate what we want students to think about (e.g., mathematics, science) so that they can learn.

Let's look at an example of the type of interactions to which we are referring. Students in a second-grade mathematics class are learning how to measure liquids. Their textbook asks them to solve the following word problem:

Katie's mother purchased an 8-ounce can of punch concentrate. How many cans will she need to create a quart of punch for Katie's birthday party?

For a student to understand this mathematical word problem, they likely need to understand the sociocultural meaning of two context-specific nouns: *concentrate* and *punch*. Otherwise they might be baffled by the sociocultural context of the word problem and not necessarily by the mathematical concepts that they are learning. Let's push this point a bit further by looking at two students in this classroom who are solving the same problem, Laura and Paul. Laura has been drinking fruit punch at home for a few years. In fact, she often accompanies her parents to the grocery store, where she helps them to purchase frozen punch concentrate in the frozen food department and then helps them to make the sweet drink when they return home. Paul, on the other hand, has never had punch or any concentrated liquids, frozen or otherwise. When they tackle the word problem, Laura completes it with ease and raises her hand in excitement to share her answer while Paul is stuck on the sociocultural meaning of the two words *concentrate* and *punch*. Hence, while he might have some understanding of mathematics, he is unfamiliar with the context in which the word problem is situated. Learning involves both a sociocultural context as well as subject-specific thinking. Figure 1.3 provides us with a visual adaptation of Vygotsky's contributions.

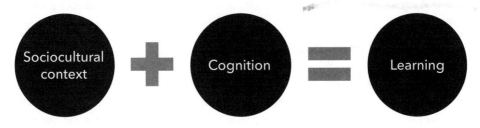

Figure 1.3: Formula for Learning *(Adapted from Vygotsky, 1978)*

While our example is situated between two American, English-speaking students, Laura and Paul, an even more obvious example is what occurs between a student who is a native speaker of the language of instruction in their school and a student who is not. Let's look at an additional example of a second-grade student, Oscar, who is in the same class as Laura and Paul. Oscar recently emigrated from Mexico, where his family worked as day laborers in agricultural work. While Oscar is a bright child who shows great promise to his parents and relatives, his lack of English and the sociocultural context of the mathematics problems in his text put him at a double disadvantage. First, he doesn't understand English and second, he has no sociocultural background or experiential knowledge of *punch concentrate*.

Oscar is an example of how our contexts (our family, family community, school community, local community, and beyond) play an essential role in how we make sense of what we experience. This is particularly true in school. As humans, we continually draw from our personal, social, cultural, linguistic, academic, and world experiences to process information, make sense of it, and learn new information. Becoming literate in one or more than one language (i.e., biliterate or multiliterate) includes our building upon these multiple processes first at the word level, then the sentence, paragraph, and chapter levels and beyond (Lesaux, Koda, Siegel & Shanahan, 2006; Pransky, 2008; Bailey & Pransky, 2003/2014).

Let's look at a quick example of this process in action. When Paul was a toddler and he was thirsty, he pointed to a bottle of juice. Paul's parent responded to his pointing by saying, "Paul, do you want juice?" Paul first responded by jumping and reaching his arms for the bottle. His parent responded to his non-verbal action by saying, "Okay, here is your bottle of juice." As Paul grew and his parent asked the same question, Paul responded with more language. At first, he said, "Juicey!" Then he said, "Want juicey!" As Paul grew to be school age and entered kindergarten for his first exposure to public school, his teacher asked him what he wanted to drink during the kindergarten's appointed snack time. When this happened, Paul responded with, "May I please have orange juice?"

As humans, we learn across all academic disciplines (e.g., mathematics, science, history, technology) by first making sense of what we are experiencing through the lens of our prior experiences *and* by engaging in a myriad of interactive social-processing skills. The example that we provided of Paul with his parent and later with his teacher describes the types of social interactions that he has grown used to having. Further, he has always been an active participant in these. This is an example of one engaging in actively processing skills. In addition, the act of processing includes a wide variety of responses from asking questions, to responding, making predictions, inferencing, expanding, analyzing, and much more. We all use these socially interactive actions to build on our ever-growing repertoire of communicating from our own personal experiences.

As such, we must also think of literacy as being situated in a sociocultural context that is as dependent on our personal, social, cultural, linguistic, academic, and world experiences as verbally communicating. In a real sense, it is the coming together of these varied and richly interactive experiences and the knowledge that we gain from them that forms what we know as literacy. While we might think of culture as something that is big, like an iconic painting drawn by a renowned artist from another country or literature or poetry penned by a famous writer from a specific culture, culture is far more complex than that. In fact, culture is the small yet nuanced action we take that reflects who we are when we communicate.

According to sociolinguist James Gee (2009), being literate in a language does not occur in isolation or in what we do on our own. Acknowledging the contributions of Vygotsky, Gee claims that literacy occurs when we socially interact with others to fully understand *and* contribute to what is occurring in the context that it is occurring. To do this well with our students, we must have depth of knowledge about their personal, social, cultural, linguistic, academic, and world experiences so that we can build from these to support them to learn and build the ever-expanding depth of subject matter and social-emotional communicative knowledge that they need to be successful learners and citizens in their classrooms, schools, communities, and more. In addition, every student must also have meaningful and continuous social interactions to learn. As you will see in our book, one teacher alone could never do this. There are too many interactions students must have with others to fully engage in the process of being socially interactive to think and to learn. To do this well, we can enlist the support of students' peers and others in our classrooms (e.g., co-teachers, classroom aides, volunteers, adult mentors, and student mentors). The key for learning to occur is ensuring that all students have meaningful and continuous interactions to learn. In other words, the more time students have to fully and nimbly interact socially and culturally in and out of school, the better.

Michael Agar (2006, 1995) coined the term *languaculture* to describe the interdependent roles that language and culture have on each other. If we think about how we use language to speak, we use it to communicate within a given social context, as we described earlier. This context drives the words that we use to convey meaning as well as understand the world around us. The same holds true for reading and writing as they, too, reflect social and cultural practices (Gee, 2010).

As an example, let's look at three different scenarios about tea. In the first example, we invite you for a cup of tea at one of our homes. You meet us at the appointed house and we enjoy a cup of tea and some cookies. The type of engagement that we have is informal with the expectation that we will converse while enjoying the beverage and refreshments. In our second example, we are writers for a prestigious scientific journal about nutrition and are writing an article about the beneficial properties of green tea. To do this well, we have to consider scientific and medical research about this type of tea as well as the writing conventions required of us to write an article of this nature. In the third scenario, each of us is a history teacher teaching our students a unit of study on the American Revolution, including the events surrounding the Boston Tea Party. We will engage our students in a historical study of this time period and create assignments and tasks that will help them to master the content expected of them. Each of these three scenarios is situated in a very different social and cultural context and require us as writers and you as readers to have depth of knowledge in these three areas to fully understand their meaning. In other words, the language that we use to listen, speak, read, and write is much more than language and, as such, the instructional programming that we build for all of our students must reflect these essential language, social, and cultural connections.

Take a few moments to complete the following two reflection activities.
Drawing from the three different examples about tea, describe how language is situated in a social and cultural context.

_____

_____

_____

Create an additional example about tea that illustrates how a concept is dependent on the social and cultural context in which it occurs.

_____

_____

_____

A Research-based Academic Language Perspective

A strategy for strengthening the instructional programming that we provide is to look more carefully at what it means to be fully competent in using the language of school. A helpful way for defining what this means is to use the federal definition of proficiency in English as it applies to English learners. While they are not the full target population of our book (as culturally responsive practices are for more than any one group), the definition can easily be applied to the general population of our nation's students. The federal definition of English proficiency is defined as the following:

- "The ability to meet the state's proficient level of achievement on state assessments.
- The ability to successfully achieve in classrooms where the language of instruction is English.

- The opportunity to participate fully in society" (U.S. Department of Education, n.d.).

The definition provides us with a blueprint of what is means to possess the academic or school language needed to be successful in school. Unfortunately, many of the groups we described earlier in this chapter include vernacular speakers of English and others who do not yet possess the academic language skills that are needed to be successful in school. That success requires that they have the following:

1. "deep cultural knowledge;
2. the ability to listen, speak, read, and write;
3. academic or subject matter knowledge; and
4. the ability to think-to-learn" in the areas being studied (Zacarian, 2015).

These represent four key elements or prongs that are required for students to be successful in school.

Many students are exposed to this type of academic language at a young age and come to school with this knowledge and these skills. Zacarian (2015) refers to this as a *literacy suitcase* that students carry to, in, and from school. For example, consider a young boy who spends his childhood observing his parents reading the newspaper, looking at recipe books, assembling grocery lists, and taking him to the local bookstore or library. If we were to listen to the conversations that his parents have with him, we would hear many open-ended questions such as "What would happen if . . . ?" These early behaviors are what we call "pre-literacy" behaviors, regardless of the language that the boy and his parents speak, and they also are what Zacarian (2015) refers to as literacy as a cultural way of being. If we consider the various groups of students that we teach, some seem to come in with this type of school or academic language while others need to acquire it.

In her work and research, Soto (2016) suggests that for English language learners (ELLs), academic language mastery is the key to accessing rigorous content. That being said, as educators, we need to understand the language assets that our students bring to school, including a primary language and/or a variation of English, and build upon those language foundations. Our goal should never be to remove a primary language or variation of English, but instead to use it to scaffold the development of academic English. Language variations and primary languages often represent culture, as language and culture are intertwined. As such, we want students to be proficient and confident in both language sets. In this way, we propose that as students acquire academic English, they should be taught how to *code switch*, or how to use the appropriate register of language for the appropriate context.

Another group of students are those who have academic language needs but are not formally identified as such and are commonly referred to as standard English learners (SELs). SELs are students who speak languages that do not correspond to standard American English language structure and grammar used in school but do incorporate English vocabulary. Among the most commonly occurring groups of students who are SELs are African American students who speak African American language (AAL), sometimes referred to as African American English, and Mexican American, non-new-immigrant students who speak Mexican American language (MxAL), or what is commonly referred to as Chicano English. ELLs and SELS need instructional assistance in the academic language necessary to be successful in school, college, and beyond. For both groups of students, academic language represents the pathway to full access in meeting the rigorous demands of the new standards.

All students can benefit from academic language development modeling, scaffolding, and practice, but ELLs and SELs need it to survive and thrive in school. ELLs have plenty of language assets in their primary language that we must leverage to grow their academic English, yet there is often a very clear language and literacy gap that must be closed as soon as ELLs enter school. Similarly, SELs come to school with a language variation that must first be understood to be built upon in the classroom setting. In reviewing the wide range of literature by experts in this field, most agree that the key elements of academic English language for ELLs and SELs include the following four dimensions: academic vocabulary, syntax and grammar, discourse, and culturally responsive teaching. The four dimensions are defined as follows:

1. Discourse—using the primary language and language variation as an asset in the classroom; using contrastive analysis as a tool for academic language development (ALD); moving from informal to formal registers of language.
2. Academic vocabulary—teaching Tier 2 (high-utility vocabulary) and Tier 3 (discipline-specific vocabulary) across content areas in an efficient manner.
3. Syntax/grammar—moving beyond basic language; teaching sophisticated and complex syntactical and grammatical structures in context to content.
4. Culturally responsive teaching—incorporating culture while addressing and teaching language, as well as honoring students' home cultures and communities.

A fundamental distinction between those who use academic language and those who do not yet is that the former has had a great amount of home and school matched academic language learning experiences. This is not to say that they do not need a program that attends to their learning needs. Rather, they are much more likely to develop the type of school language needed more quickly than students who have not had this experience. We must think carefully about the instruction and instructional practices we employ so that they provide all of our students—those who come to school with school matched language skills and those who have not had the privilege of this experience—with ample and effective opportunities to acquire these skills and be able to use them independently. To do this well, we have to consider the usage of the following four prongs drawn from Zacarian's (2015) research and writing on this topic.

Learning as a Sociocultural Process

First, we must connect learning to our students' personal, social, cultural, and world knowledge. While we might think of this as building from our students' backgrounds, we have to consider it from a cultural perspective. Many students from underrepresented populations come from cultures in which group harmony, relationships, and collectivism take priority over independence (DeCapua & Marshall, 2010; Hofstede, 2001; Hofstede & Hofstede, 2005). As such, we must engage in the following relationship-building efforts to match the collectivist cultures of an increasingly diverse student and family populace: build strong relationships with students, intentionally help students to build strong relationships with each other, create activities that engage families, the school community and the community-at-large, and connect the curriculum to issues that are socially relevant to students (Zacarian, 2013/2015).

Learning Academic Language as a Development Process

Second, we must also understand literacy as a developmental process that is dependent on a student's age, prior literacy learning experiences and, most importantly, exposure to and apprenticeship into literacy practices. That being said, we must begin with the premise that all students bring with them language foundations that can be built upon. In this sense, students must be mentored into this essential way of being through repeated and continuous activities that support the type of communication that is required of them in school. While this means rich exposure to vocabulary and language functions and conventions, it requires that students have the opportunity to build vocabulary, print, and context knowledge (Lesaux, Koda, Siegel, & Shanahan, 2006). This building can only occur through repeated exposure and, most importantly, practice using language to communicate. To do this requires that we create a highly interactive environment where students have multiple and continuous opportunities to use language.

We also cannot underestimate the power of spoken language and its influence on reading and writing. For ELLs, academic oral language is the foundation of literacy (Lesaux & Shanahan, 2006). Therefore, ELLs must use and practice academic oral language daily. This means that teachers must intentionally plan for and incorporate academic oral language across a school day. Teachers should be gradually releasing speaking responsibilities to their students during every content area block, as most students, especially ELLs, make personal meaning through academic talk. In addition, we have to help students understand how language works in context. For example, a science experiment is written much differently than an historical piece or grocery list. We must help our students understand how language is used in specific contexts and, importantly, what an author's intent is in having language function in this way (Pransky, 2008; Fang & Schleppegrell, 2010). For example, if a historian is writing a piece about the Civil War, much of the language will be written in the past tense and will take place in a certain context (e.g., a Southern battlefield that was far away from a Northerner's home). Each subject matter discipline has its own way of communicating, and we must consider ourselves as language teachers of this content (Freeman & Freeman, 2009; Richards, 2015; Hammer, Viesca, and Commons, 2019).

Learning as an Academic Process

Each subject matter has its own content vocabulary (Calderón & Minaye-Rowe, 2010). If we return, for example, to the study of the Civil War, we see terms such as *Confederation, abolitionist, battalion,* and *Confederate States.* All students must learn this vocabulary in school, as it is not likely that they will be exposed to it outside of school. If we provide students with challenging and thought-provoking activities that center on the content and are of student interest, we have a much better chance of their learning the academic language content. To do this well, we must provide many modeling and practice opportunities of the thinking process and procedures necessary for students to engage in these activities.

Learning as a Cognitive Process

Two important skills that are required of all learners is the ability to understand a learning task and engage in it meaningfully. Students who possess academic language are more likely to be able to understand the thinking behind a learning task and have the capacity to engage in it. In this sense, they are able to use their thinking skills to learn. For example, in the same social studies lesson, the teacher assigns the following letter-writing task: *Describe what your character is experiencing in the Civil War and what they decide to share about it with a loved one.* Some students understand the thinking process behind this task, whereas others need a good deal of support to engage in it successfully. As effective teachers, we must support our students in this thinking-to-learn process.

To be an active learner means that we have time to understand the rules, systems, and conventions of our learning communities (Gee, 2009). Some students already understand these systems of thinking as they have had many life experiences with them and can draw from them to engage in the learning tasks we assign. Others have not had this experience and need to be apprenticed into it.

Consider what we have shared about some of the features of a student who possesses school language. What are some of the social and cultural contextual understandings that student would need to have to be successful in mathematics? _____

_____

_____

_____

Consider the four prongs that we introduced: learning is a sociocultural, academically, literacy, and cognitively developmental process.

    a. What do you or would you do to be sure that you are connecting to students' prior personal, cultural, and world experiences?

       _____

       _____

       _____

    b. What steps might you take to learn about the literacy learning of students?

       _____

       _____

       _____

    c. What are one to two steps that you might take to support students' understanding of how a particular subject matter language is presented?

       _____

       _____

       _____

    d. What are one to two steps you might take to help students to think as learners?

       _____

       _____

       _____

One of the key overarching levers for ensuring that we are using practices that match our students' academic and social-emotional language and learning needs is the usage of culturally responsive teaching pedagogy. Further, it is ensuring that we use this in all that we do to plan, implement, reflect upon, and evaluate the effectiveness of our work with students and partnerships with their families. An important lens for understanding the urgency for using this approach is the founding mothers of culturally responsive teaching: Geneva Gay and Gloria Ladson-Billings. In our next section, we present their seminal contributions.

WHAT ARE THE KEY THEORETICAL UNDERPINNINGS FOR CULTURALLY RESPONSIVE TEACHING?

Geneva Gay (2010) defines culturally responsive teaching as "using the cultural knowledge, prior experiences, frames of reference, and performance styles of ethnically diverse students to make learning encounters more relevant to and effective for [students]" (p. 31). Similarly, Gloria Ladson-Billings (1994) suggests that culturally responsive teaching is "a pedagogy that empowers students intellectually, socially, emotionally, and politically [because it uses] cultural referents to impart knowledge, skills, and attitudes" (p. 20). As such, teachers who utilize a culturally responsive method in their teaching view culture as an asset, which can be used effectively to enhance academic and social achievement. The concept of culture as an asset looks closely at what all students bring to the work of learning as opposed to what we might erroneously presume they don't.

In her theory of culturally relevant teaching, Ladson-Billings (1995) outlines two key theoretical underpinnings that are critical to the development of culturally relevant pedagogy:

- *sociocultural consciousness*, which Ladson-Billings generally refers to as conceptions of self and others; and
- *caring for students* which expands beyond caring about students' academic well-being to a holistic focus on their overall needs coupled with having high expectations of them.

Having established these two theoretical underpinnings of *sociocultural consciousness* and *caring* as prerequisites of culturally relevant pedagogy, Ladson-Billings (1995) then outlines three central tenets of this type of constructivist equity pedagogy, as follows:

- **High expectations:** Culturally relevant teaching emphasizes academic success for all students.
- **Cultural competence:** Culturally relevant teaching assists students in the formation of a positive cultural identity.

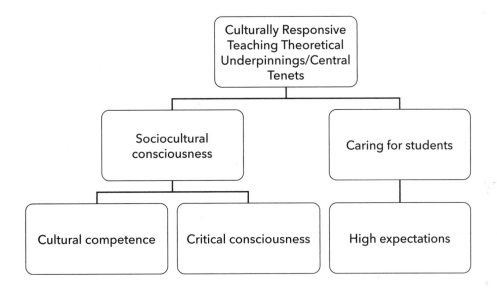

Figure 1.4: Culturally Responsive Teaching Theory and Central Tenets *(Adapted from Ladson-Billings, 1995)*

- **Critical consciousness:** Culturally relevant teaching guides students in developing a critical consciousness they can use to critique or interrupt current and historical social inequities.

As Ladson-Billings (1995) suggests, "I have defined culturally relevant teaching as a pedagogy of opposition, not unlike critical pedagogy but specifically committed to collective, not merely individual empowerment." Figure 1.4 visually demonstrates how Ladson-Billings' theoretical underpinnings and central tenets intersect.

Take a few moments to complete the following reflection activities.

1. Describe the key differences between sociocultural consciousness and caring for students.

   _____

   _____

   _____

   _____

2. How might these differences be evidenced in a classroom setting?

   _____

   _____

   _____

   _____

SYNTHESIS OF CULTURALLY RESPONSIVE PEDAGOGY IMPLEMENTATION RESEARCH

A synthesis of classroom-based research on the implementation of culturally relevant pedagogy by Kristan A. Morrison, Holly H. Robbins, and Dana Gregory Rose (2008) generated 45 research studies from 1995 to 2008 and highlighted culturally relevant pedagogy as enacted in classrooms. The research studies were then categorized into Ladson-Billings' three tenets of culturally responsive teaching—*high expectations*, *cultural competence*, and *critical consciousness*.

High Expectations

Some of the research study themes that emerged from the high expectations tenet included:

- **Modeling, scaffolding, and clarification of challenging curriculum:** Some of the ways that culturally responsive teachers demonstrate high expectations is via their willingness to model, scaffold, and clarify challenging curriculum. Culturally responsive teachers explicitly model rigorous concepts or thinking process, and they realize that scaffolds are necessary but also temporary assistance that should eventually be taken away when a rigorous concept has been internalized (Soto, 2012).
- **Using students' strengths as instructional starting points:** Culturally responsive teachers utilize an asset-based model of instruction instead of focusing on deficits. Such teachers realize that their students want to be viewed by and are motivated from their strengths, and they know how to build upon those strengths to close any gaps that may exist. Further, we cannot and should not undermine the critical concept of supporting students to feel safe, a sense of belonging, value, and competent. These four essentials greatly help all students to become active learners (Zacarian, Alvarez-Ortiz and Haynes, 2017).
- **Investing and taking personal responsibility for students' success:** Culturally responsive teachers make their students' success a personal goal. In other words, if their students are not succeeding, then these teachers feel as if they are not succeeding. They will not rest or give up until all of their students are successful. Part of this motivation comes from finding our own voice as teachers and in giving our students a voice and choice in their own learning.
- **Creating and nurturing cooperative environments:** Since culturally responsive teaching is, as Ladson-Billings suggests, "specifically committed to collective, not merely individual empowerment," teaching students how to work coop-

eratively and democratically must be integrated within the classroom setting. Students will need to be taught how to work with each other so that interdependence is the goal. Each person in a group must have an equal role, and expectations for group work need to be clear (Soto, 2012; Zacarian, 2013).

- **High behavioral expectations:** Just as culturally responsive teachers have high expectations for academic achievement, they also have high expectations for student behavior. Students should be explicitly taught how to regulate their behavior so that they are able to focus on their academic expectations. A key aspect of this is that they develop the social-emotional language that is needed to engage interactively and interdependently with others in the classroom and beyond (Zacarian & Silverstone, 2020).

Cultural Competence

Ladson-Billings (1995) suggests that the goal of culturally relevant teaching is not to have students achieve and acquire the norms of the dominant culture. Instead, culturally relevant pedagogy *must* develop in students a sense of cultural competence, a "dynamic or synergistic relationship between home/community culture and school culture" (Ladson-Billings, 1995, p. 467). Examples of cultural competence include reshaping the prescribed curriculum, building on students' funds of knowledge, and establishing relationships between school and the children's homes. Reshaping the prescribed curriculum refers to ensuring that the curriculum is connected to students' ethnic, linguistic, and cultural backgrounds. In other words, the curriculum should build to and from students' experiences. Similarly, the curriculum should build upon students' prior and background knowledge as well as their *funds of knowledge* (González, Moll, and Amanti, 2005). *All* students bring to the table prior or background knowledge, even if it doesn't match American or classroom expectations for such knowledge. Instead, a culturally responsive teacher's responsibility is to understand, utilize, and leverage the funds of knowledge that students bring to school and then fill in any areas where additional background knowledge can be taught or experienced. One way to build on students' funds of knowledge is to establish relationships between school and children's homes. Since students' homes and communities are what they know best, it is essential that we bring their homes and communities into the classroom in meaningful ways. This may include more communal classroom configurations, such as productive group work, which can mirror home, or intentionally bringing in parents or community members who can be guest speakers or provide internships (i.e., if they work in the community and/or a trade field that students are interested in) (Soto, 2012). It may also include meeting with parents/guardians for the sole purpose of building reciprocal relationships with them and demonstrating that we are caring professionals who are committed to partnering with families in all that we do as educators. The list below shows the type of questions that are intended for this relationship-building purpose.

Figure 1.5: Partnership Meetings with Parents/Guardians

1. What makes [name of child] special in terms of their qualities, and what sets them apart from others?
2. What are some things you enjoy about [name of child]?
3. What are [name of child]'s particular talents or skills?
4. What are things you enjoy doing as a family?
5. We want our school to be a welcoming place for all parents. What might help to make you or someone you know feel more welcome?
6. We welcome parents as partners. Is there any particular way that you would like to help me to make your child's experience a great one?
7. What special talents or interests would you consider sharing with your child's class or with other families?
8. What are your child's hopes and dreams and/or your hopes and dreams for your child?
9. What questions do you wish I had asked and would like to be sure are included?

(Adapted from Zacarian, Alvarez-Ortiz & Haynes, 2017)

Critical Consciousness

Ladson-Billings (1995) asserts, "not only must teachers encourage academic success and cultural competence, they must help students to recognize, understand, and critique current social inequities" (p. 476). The research study themes for this culturally responsive teaching tenet included critical literacy, as described by Luke (2000), where students are invited to question, examine, and even dispute the power relations between writers and readers. The other way that the critical consciousness tenet emerged in the analysis of research included "preparing students for acting upon issues of social justice, preparing them for the power dynamics of mainstream society, and empowering students within this society" (Morrison, Robbins, & Rose, 2008, p. 441). The latter might include engaging students in social justice work in their communities, where they might see and attempt to solve an inequity in their community. Studies in this vein also suggested that culturally responsive teachers worked to make explicit the power dynamics of mainstream society and shared power in the classroom. For example, a culturally responsive teacher might choose to provide a unit on the Black Lives Matter movement to highlight and figure out ways to challenge police brutality in their own communities. Culturally responsive teachers might also choose to have more egalitarian and inclusive power dynamics in the classroom setting, where students have a voice and choice in terms of behavioral and academic expectations. Part of this stance is to support students to apprentice into understanding issues of critical importance in their local, state, national, and global communities and to seek ways in which they can be empowered to contribute (Zacarian and Silverstone, 2020).

GENEVA GAY'S SIX DIMENSIONS OF CULTURALLY RESPONSIVE TEACHING

Geneva Gay (2010), founding mother of culturally responsive teaching theory, research, and practice, suggests, "Culturally responsive teaching can be defined as using cultural knowledge, prior experiences, frames of reference, and performance styles of ethnically diverse students to make learning encounters more relevant and effective for them. It teaches *to and through* the strengths of these students. Culturally responsive teaching is the behavioral expression of knowledge, beliefs, and values that recognize the importance of racial and cultural diversity in learning." According to Gay, culturally responsive teaching rests on six dimensions:

- Culturally responsive teachers are socially and academically empowering by setting high expectations for students with a commitment to every student's success;
- Culturally responsive teachers are *multidimensional* because they engage cultural knowledge, experiences, contributions, and perspectives;
- Culturally responsive teachers *validate every student's culture*, bridging gaps between school and home through diversified instructional strategies and multicultural curricula;
- Culturally responsive teachers are *socially, emotionally, and politically comprehensive* as they seek to educate the whole child;
- Culturally responsive teachers are *transformative of schools and societies* by using students' existing strengths to drive instruction, assessment, and curriculum design; Culturally responsive teachers are *emancipatory and liberating from oppressive educational practices and ideologies* as they lift "the veil of presumed absolute authority from conceptions of scholarly truth typically taught in schools." (Gay, 2010, p. 38)

Associated with the six dimensions of culturally responsive teaching are the four practical actions that Gay (2013) believes are essential to implementing culturally responsive teaching. These include:

Practical actions:

- replacing deficit perspectives of students and communities;
- understanding the resistance to culturally responsive teaching from critics so they are more confident and competent in implementation (e.g., having teachers conduct their own analysis of textbooks to investigate how different knowledge forms affect teaching and learning);
- understanding how and why culture and difference are essential ideologies for culturally responsive teaching given they are essential to humanity; and
- making pedagogical connections within the context in which they are teaching.

Figure 1.6 visually demonstrates the intersection between Gay's four essential actions for culturally responsive teaching alongside Ladson-Billings' central tenets of culturally responsive teaching.

Gay's Four Essential Actions for Culturally Responsive Teaching (2013)	Ladson-Billings' Culturally Responsive Teaching Central Tenets (1995)
• Replacing deficit perspectives of students and communities	• High Expectations
• Understanding the resistance to culturally responsive teaching from critics so they are more confident and competent in implementation	• Critical Consciousness
• Understanding how and why culture and difference are essential ideologies for culturally responsive teaching given they are essential to humanity	• Cultural Competence
• Making pedagogical connections within the context in which they are teaching	• High Expectations

Figure 1.6: Intersection Between Gay's Four Essential Actions and Ladson-Billings' Central Tenets

Take a few moments to respond to the following questions.
1. On a scale of 1–5 (1 being lowest and 5 being highest), where do you see yourself along Gay's Four Essential Actions for Culturally Responsive Teaching and Ladson-Billings' Culturally Responsive Teaching Tenets?

_____

_____

_____

2. What are your goals and next steps with culturally responsive teaching?

_____

_____

_____

CLASSROOM MANIFESTATIONS OF CULTURALLY RESPONSIVE TEACHING

According to Teel and Obidah (2008), culturally responsive teaching then manifests itself in the classroom setting based on a set of racial and cultural competencies. They include:

- seeing cultural differences as assets—cultural difference should be leveraged in the classroom setting and utilized as often as necessary;
- creating caring learning communities where individuals from diverse cultures and heritages are valued—students and teachers should be taught to respect cultural and heritage differences by creating communal and inclusive learning environments where every voice is democratically valued;
- using cultural knowledge of ethnically diverse cultures, families, and communities to guide curriculum development, classroom climates, instructional strategies, and relationships with students—students understand that they are valued as they see themselves in the curriculum and via culturally responsive pedagogies that are inclusive;
- challenging racial and cultural stereotypes, prejudices, racism, and other forms of intolerance, injustice, and oppression—students read about and learn how to challenge societal and personal implicit biases and forms of oppression;
- being change agents for social justice and academic equity—students learn to apply equitable and inclusive principles in their own lives and in their communities;

- mediating power imbalances in classrooms based on race, culture, ethnicity, and class—students learn about power dynamics in their classroom and in society, and teachers work to create more egalitarian and democratic spaces; and
- accepting cultural responsiveness as endemic to educational effectiveness in all areas of learning for students from all ethnic groups—cultural responsiveness will positively affect *all* students, as all students learn more effectively in a setting that is inclusive of every part of themselves.

There are many other culturally responsive theorists that we could have referred to in this section, but we chose Ladson-Billings and Gay because of their theoretical intersections, as well as their practical focus on instruction and direct application to the classroom setting. Our goal is to have these theoretical underpinnings guide the rest of the content in this book by making direct connections to them in each chapter.

2

Understanding Identity as Socially and Interactionally Constructed

WHEN RENOWNED SOCIOLOGIST and Harvard professor Sarah Lawrence-Lightfoot, the first African American to have an endowed professorship named in her honor, was seven years old and in the second grade, she contracted an illness that prevented her from attending school for three months. While convalescing, she was home schooled by her maternal grandmother, a former teacher, who Lawrence-Lightfoot describes as being stricter and more rigorous than any teacher she's experienced in her lifetime. When she recovered, she vividly recalls her return to school and how special it was when her second-grade teacher accompanied her to await her parents' arrival to bring her home. That feeling disappeared the second that her teacher spoke to her parents. Here is Lawrence-Lightfoot's recollection of that remarkably powerful experience:

> She did not think that there was any way that I could make up for lost time; it would, therefore, be necessary for me to repeat the second grade. But that wasn't the worst of what Mrs. Sullivan had to say. She also thought that my parents had to face the fact that I "might not be college material." *(Lawrence-Lightfoot, 2003, p. xii-xvii)*

She recounts how angry she was that her parents did not respond to tell her teacher how smart and capable she was. Her father, a professor of sociology who specialized in "Black activism in the South," and her mother said nothing to her teacher.

Rather, they waited till they returned home to tell her that "the best way to prove her [teacher] wrong was for me to do excellent work (Lawrence-Lightfoot, 2003, xv)."

When Lynn Pelkey was 35 years old and working toward a bachelor's degree in hotel management, she wrote an essay about what it felt like to be a person with a learning disability [LD] and to live in the culture of what she refers as an "LD bubble . . . isolated and separated from 'normals' during her elementary and secondary years when she frequently overheard teachers describe her as 'not doing as well as other children . . . having difficulty . . . scoring low, not trying . . . and being lazy' " (Pelkey, 2001, pp. 17–19). These declarations affirmed for Pelky that she was not just different from her peers; she was "less than" them. That feeling of inferiority plagued her throughout her childhood and adult years despite some of the experiences that countered her self-perception. Two of these occurred when she was in seventh grade. The first experience happened when she was slowly walking a friend to her algebra class and hanging around the outside of that classroom to avoid having to go to the "remedial room," or what she and others referred to as the "retard room," an experience that Pelkey found wholly negative. While standing outside of her peers' class, the algebra teacher surprisingly asked Pelkey to join her friend. Without hesitation, she walked into the algebra class. Here is Pelkey's recollection of the experience:

> . . . something magical happened to me. I could understand what he was teaching. I was learning. I wasn't memorizing, I was thinking, and I was figuring out the answer. I was learning. This was one of the first experiences that shot a pinhole in the bubble that trapped me in my LDness. *(Pelkey, 2001, p. 21)*

Later that year, she missed many months of school to have corrective surgeries for a birth defect. Like Lawrence-Lightfoot, she vividly remembers returning to school, where she went to the school library and worked with a tutor who helped her to catch up. Here is her recollection of a conversation that she had with the tutor:

> She talked directly to me about my disability. She explained it like this. "Lynn, you are part of a minority, a small portion of the population that has a learning disability. You and others like you learn a certain way. The rest of the people learn another way. . . . You are truly special because you have stretched your brain and learning beyond and outside of your disabilities, and this is something that the majority has not had to do." *(Pelkey, 2001, p. 22)*

These two experiences, however, did not have an impact on Pelkey's poor perception of herself as a learner during her public school years. It wasn't until many years later, when she went to an open house at a local community college with the encouragement of her mother, that she reluctantly enrolled and found that she was, indeed, a capable and successful learner.

Lawrence-Lightfoot's and Pelkey's recollections of the interactions they had and observations they made during their school years speak strongly about the profound power of personal experiences and the influence that deficit-based interactions and low expectations versus having and holding high expectations have in shaping our various and diverse identities. The two student examples present a compelling argument against the usage of deficit-based assumptions and perceptions of our students. As we will explore in this chapter, culturally responsive practices and pedagogy require that we shine a light on the goodness, strengths, and assets of our students and their families to support the potential of students' developing a positive self-image or identity and an asset-based view of their academic and social-emotional development.

We begin our chapter with a presentation of seminal research in the area of *expectation theory*, as it is foundational to much of the research that has emerged more recently in this arena. We then continue to explore key concepts of cultural responsiveness by defining cultural identity as expressed through the language that we use to communicate, in various social contexts, our and others' identities and ways of being and acting. We also describe child development as involving repeated and continuous interactions that a child observes or engages with and among their parents or guardians, family, family's community, school community, and the local community in which the child is reared. We discuss how each of these richly diverse interactional events supports the development of a child's personal, cultural, social, and world views and identity. Drawing from seminal child psychologist Mary Gauvain (2001) and Barbara Rogoff (1990; 2003), we also discuss how the social and interactional settings children are raised and schooled in can provide both positive and constraining opportunities for development. We also draw from the framework about cultural responsiveness that we presented in our first chapter to show the importance of using a strengths-based approach in which we see students as highly competent and enact practices that reinforce their competencies as well as their feeling of being viewed and recognized as competent learners.

WHAT DOES EXPECTATION THEORY HAVE TO DO WITH CULTURAL RESPONSIVENESS?

Research reported by Dusek and Joseph (1986) suggests that African American and Mexican American students were not expected to perform as well as White students by their teachers. Expectations are often communicated to students by teachers in either covert or overt ways. According to Brophy (1983), students of teachers with low expectations exhibit the following characteristics:

1. **being called on less frequently**—students of color are oftentimes called upon less frequently by teachers. Due to this, some students may either begin to disengage in the classroom setting and/or become passive learners. Many times, this is also when we begin to see classroom management issues. We can counter this issue by requiring all students to respond to teacher prompts via strategies like think-pair-share or the use of equity sticks;

2. **when called on, provided less time to respond**—in the classroom setting, ELL students, or students who are struggling, may need more time to process information and formulate a response. ELLs, for example, are doing double the work of processing language and content, so they need both more thinking and waiting time;

3. **given the answer rather than helped to solve the problem themselves**—many times, with good intent, teachers who teach students of color or ELLs may become uncomfortable when their students cannot complete a response. This is oftentimes called the "pobrecito" ("poor thing" in Spanish) syndrome. Teachers oftentimes also unknowingly require shorter responses (called the Initiation-Response-Feedback approach), where the teacher prompts with a close-ended question, the student responds in one or two words, and the conversation is over. Instead, Gibbons (2016) recommends Teacher Guided Reporting, where the teacher initiates with an open-ended question and then uses a series of language scaffolds to extend responses;

4. **criticized more often**—either implicitly or explicitly, teachers might unknowingly criticize student behavior or performance, instead of building on assets that all students bring to the table;

5. **praised less**—students of color, who perhaps don't have an academic identity, might unknowingly be acknowledged for accomplishments less often, which can create a cycle of continued disengagement and lack of respect; and

6. **paid less positive attention but disciplined more strictly**—there is much research on how disproportionately African American boys, in particular, are written up for discipline issues in the classroom setting. Such disproportionality begins as early as kindergarten.

Similarly, anthropologist John Ogbu (1985), renowned for his contributions of theories and practices related to the challenges of underrepresented populations, states that minority students' low achievement is often due to how they are treated educationally, socially, politically, and economically. At its most basic, Ogbu's *cultural-ecological theory* of minority student performance, which we will address again in a later chapter, posits there are two sets of factors influencing minority school performance: how society at large and the school treats minorities (the system) and how minority groups respond to those treatments and to schooling (community forces). The theory further posits that differences in school performance between immigrant and non-immigrant minorities are partly due to differences in their community forces" (Ogbu, 1999, p. 156). If, as Ogbu suggests, students perceive low expectations and rewards for academic engagement and achievement, they are more likely to become discouraged from persisting and engaging in school.

As you read Brophy and Ogbu's work regarding how low expectations manifest themselves in the classroom setting:

1. How do you see yourself explicitly countering any or all of these behaviors?

_____

_____

_____

2. What are some tangible ways that you can replace low expectations with high expectations?

_____

_____

_____

IDENTITY DEVELOPMENT AS AN INTERACTIVE AND PARTICIPATORY PROCESS

In our first chapter, we drew from Geneva Gay's definition of culturally responsive teaching as "using the cultural knowledge, experiences, frames of reference, and performance styles of ethnically diverse students to make learning encounters more relevant to and effective for students" (2010). We also drew from Ladson-Billings (1995) to describe the act of caring for students as expanding beyond students' academic well-being to a holistic focus on their overall needs coupled with our high expectations of them. With this as our framework, let's engage in the following reflection activities. We will do this first for Lawrence-Lightfoot, followed by Lynn Pelkey, and conclude the segment with a reflection about ourselves. We begin with Lawrence-Lightfoot.

As you read the exchange between Sarah Lawrence-Lightfoot's teacher, Mrs. Sullivan, and her parents, what did you notice that supported or constrained Lawrence-Lightfoot's:

1. Return to school after a long absence?

_____

_____

_____

_____

2. Capacity to feel safe, a sense of belonging, valued, and competent in her second-grade setting?

_____

_____

_____

3. Perception of her teacher's caring for her?

_____

_____

_____

In our first chapter, we also discussed some key concepts of culturally responsive practices. The first is that learning occurs in a sociocultural context in which students are also supported to engage in a thinking process. We also discussed the critical importance of creating an environment where five conditions are ever present. These include that students feel safe, a sense of belonging, valued, and competent, and that they are socially responsive to others and society itself. Students' developing identities require our creating these essential conditions.

Lawrence-Lightfoot's example provides two powerful deficit-based moments in her life that are emblazoned in her memory: (1) The moment where she overheard disparaging and downright harming words about her capacities and (2) the silence that ensued when she expected her parents to respond to her teacher by defending her as a strong and capable student. Her teacher's damning declaration was, in Lawrence-Lightfoot's words, "shocking news, so unfair, so wrongheaded," and her parents' silence was equally disturbing (p. xiv). It wasn't until 35 years after this experience that Lawrence-Lightfoot's mother spoke with her and said, "I still feel guilty for not having done more to protect you from her" (p. xv). While we might argue in many ways that Mrs. Sullivan was wrong and racist, the reality is that culturally responsive practices require us to think anew about all of what we say and do on behalf of our students. Why do we say this?

Many of our practices may be subtle or assumptive about our students without really taking the time to think about their potential impacts and ensure that these five essential conditions are met. Let's say, for a hypothetical example, that the following summer, Sarah Lawrence-Lightfoot's family moves her to a new school district where she is the only African-American student. The new school receives her report card. In it, Mrs. Sullivan has given her an incomplete in all of her subject matters as she was absent for three months. You attend a meeting about the grade placement of Lawrence-Lightfoot and a colleague mentions that "students from that particular part of your state are better off repeating a grade."

Take a few moments to jot down your thoughts and ideas about this colleague's reply and the actions that you would take (or would like to take) in response. _____

_____

_____

_____

_____

_____

_____

CambellJones, CambellJones, and Lindsey (2010) refer to the type of reflection-task-challenge that we just posed as a moral dilemma–type task that often leads to a right or wrong response. They also point to how our response might be guided or affirmed by the legal cases that we cited in our first chapter as a way to point to what we perceive as a very clear response of yes or no. Foundational to our framework of cultural responsiveness is that we must be guided by an intentional process of careful and continuous examination about the ever-changing diversity of our student and family populations and of society itself to find the solutions. Further, the interactions that we witness or that we participate in may not be as explicit and overt as the hypothetical reflection task that we just furnished about Lawrence-Lightfoot. An example would be a colleague at the same hypothetical meeting about Lawrence-Lightfoot who says: "Students who have missed three months of school are better off repeating a grade." Regardless, as educators, we must continuously:

- be curious to learn about the students and families with whom we work by enacting the type of strengths-based partnership efforts that we discussed in our first chapter;
- be empathetic;
- adopt the four essential conditions of a culture of caring; and
- use sociocultural consciousness about ourselves and others.

These actions greatly support us to look for students' cultural competencies and support them to see these in themselves, perceive the inequities that are occurring in their lives and in others' lives to develop an empowered critical conscience and create instructional programming that has high expectations. Lawrence-Lightfoot's recollection of her second-grade experience demonstrates for us that her teacher did not possess and enact the central tenets of cultural responsiveness.

Enacting culturally responsive practices requires our thinking carefully and deeply about all of our interactions about and on behalf of students *and* acknowledging and identifying behaviors or interactions that might be more subtly and less obviously deficit-based. An example of the type of subtlety we are referring to is Lynn Pelkey. Lynn was diagnosed with dyslexia when she was a public school student and received services in a classroom devoted to students with disabilities. Let's look back at Pelkey by engaging in some reflection activities.

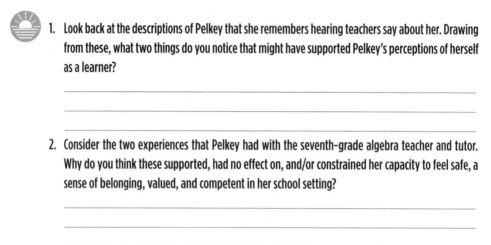

1. Look back at the descriptions of Pelkey that she remembers hearing teachers say about her. Drawing from these, what two things do you notice that might have supported Pelkey's perceptions of herself as a learner?

   _____

   _____

   _____

2. Consider the two experiences that Pelkey had with the seventh-grade algebra teacher and tutor. Why do you think these supported, had no effect on, and/or constrained her capacity to feel safe, a sense of belonging, valued, and competent in her school setting?

   _____

   _____

   _____

In our first chapter and this one, we discussed various elements of a culturally responsive approach whereby we care for the well-being of our students with a method that takes into account what Ladson-Billings (2005) refers to as a holistic approach to students' overall needs. Students with identified disabilities are particularly vulnerable to our losing sight of that holistic concept, especially and particularly when their day is fragmented and separated from the general population. It is not a matter of our simply adapting instruction to meet the learning needs of our students. For example, let's say that when Pelkey went to the remedial classroom, her teacher created an individualized lesson that precisely was created for students with dyslexia, and she excitedly and passionately provided Pelkey with this instruction. *Would Pelkey have felt less isolated from her peers?* The same question applies to any student who receives supports or instruction in addition to what is provided to the general student population. This includes thousands of students, including English learners and those receiving Title 1 services, reading support, and more.

It is questions such as this one about how a student feels when they are isolated from peers that are critical for us to ask. What we are referring to are practices that highlight our students' positive capacities and competencies so that they see these in themselves and can acknowledge and value them to continuously build a positive self-image.

We might find that Pelkey's feelings and perceptions about her lack of capacities and competencies resonate with some of our own personal experiences. Take a few moments to engage in the following reflection task about your own personal experience in school and how the experience strengthened or constrained your perception of yourself.

1. **Think of an interactional experience that you had as a student in a school setting. Describe how that experience strengthened or constrained your perception of yourself.**

_____

_____

_____

2. **How did the people involved in that interactional event support or constrain your perception of yourself?**

_____

_____

_____

DEVELOPMENT AS A CULTURAL PROCESS

As educators, whether we are aware of it consciously or unconsciously, the varied and diverse collection of interactional experiences of our students forms what we know as their individual identities. And, the interactional nature of all human existence begins at birth. Let's look at the seminal contributions of developmental psychologist Mary Gauvain (2001) and cognitive development scholar Barbara Rogoff (1990; 2003) to explain what we mean by the influence of interactions on child development. Gauvain describes one of the most unique aspects of the human species. What is it? It is that we are entirely *physically dependent* on older and more mature members of humankind for a longer period of time than any other species (Gauvain, 2001. p. 6). Further, all children, regardless of their diverse backgrounds (e.g., race, language, culture, country of origin, economic circumstances, religion), are guided to become participants in their home and family community by observing the interactions that occur in their home and outside of their home (e.g., church, in the market) *and* actively being guided, coached, and explicitly and implicitly coaxed to interactively participate with others. Let's look at what we mean.

A child is born. During the first weeks of life and for much longer, the child's physical needs are constantly and continuously cared for by its parents or guardians. Whether the child is living with two parents, a single parent, a foster parent, or extrafamilial supports, it is these close interactions, both physical and emotional, that cement the parent–child bond. Other people living in the home, such as siblings, grandparents, and others, are also a part of a child's interactional routines and bonding experiences. For example, when a baby is hungry, the baby cries. Within minutes, the baby's parent or caregiver lovingly attends to the baby's need by holding and feeding the baby. As the baby grows, it begins to interact with others with more frequency at home and in the family's community, such as the local stores that the family shops or religious institutions the family attends. Throughout the routine observations and interactional experiences that children engage in, they each learn how to act according to the meaning that they acquire and derive from the world around them and the cultural rules that govern it. Let's say, for example, that we have the privilege of observing the bedtime rituals of three different four-year-old children: Mateo, Lucy, and Anna.

Three Examples of Identity Development as a Cultural Process

Mateo is a monolingual, Spanish-speaking child whose parents are middle-class graduate students. His father is studying mechanical and his mother biomedical engineering at a large university setting in California. Both of his parents are highly literate and believe that reading to their child, Mateo, is critical to his success as a learner. Each night, one of his parents typically reads aloud in Spanish two of his favorite picture books about dinosaurs. He loves this activity so much that he brings the books to the parent who engages in this nightly bedtime ritual with him by telling him that it is time for bed. "Si, es tiempo para dormirse," one of his parents says as they guide him to his room. During the weekdays, Mateo is cared for by a Spanish-speaking childcare provider. On the weekends, Mateo's parents take him regularly to the children's, art, and science museums as well as the local aquarium. They often are accompanied by fellow Spanish-speaking graduate students and their children. Mateo's family also frequents bookstores and the local library, as many literacy-oriented families do, where Mateo adds to his ever-growing assortment of books about dinosaurs. If we had the opportunity to stand nearby his parents and observe their interactions with Mateo at the art museum, we would hear them asking open-ended questions in Spanish. Translated into English, these include such questions as: "Do you think that painting looks like our community? How is it different? How it is the same?" They ask questions such as these to support Mateo in developing the thinking skills (e.g., analyzing, comparing, contrasting) that they believe he will need in the future when he attends school.

Lucy lives with her grandmother in a rural community in South Carolina. At bedtime, after Lucy has brushed her teeth, taken a bath, and put on her pajamas, her grandmother tucks her into her bed and sings bedtime songs. They have been doing this bedtime ritual since Lucy was a baby. Lucy is always encouraged to request the first song and she always asks for one that they have sung at church. The second song always involves a sing-along like "Row, Row, Row Your Boat" that her grandmother has taught her to sing. Lucy knows the perfect timing involved in singing a round and carefully blends her voice to match the rhythm of her grandmother. During the day, Lucy accompanies her grandmother to the local shops where they buy the day's groceries and her grandmother gets her hair done. Religion plays a prominent role in their lives. During the week, they regularly visit with members of their church. Wednesday afternoons include a bible study at their home with older church members, and Sundays are devoted to attending services and post-church lunches. Lucy has observed and participated in these daily and weekly rituals throughout her young life and is known and beloved by her family community.

Anna currently lives in a homeless shelter. For years, her parents have worked multiple minimum-wage jobs and lived in a variety of low-income settings in the same urban community. For the past few weeks, they have been living in two different homeless shelters—one for males (where her father is staying) and the other for females (where her mother, sister, and Anna are staying). This is the first time that the family has had to live in a publicly supervised and operated shelter. Despite their tenuous living circumstances, Anna's parents have always tried to support her to fall asleep by telling her a bedtime story about their own childhoods. She is so familiar with these that she often requests they tell her about a particular childhood experience of theirs, such as the time that her father's parents searched for him when he got lost at a department store and the time her mother and aunt were playing and broke her grandmother's favorite vase. While staying at the shelter, her mother is doing her best to adhere to the same bedtime ritual with which Anna is familiar. If we were nearby them in the shelter, we would hear the following:

ANNA: "Tell me the vase story!"

ANNA'S MOTHER: "Oh, that's a good one. My sister dropped it alright."

ANNA: "Yes, that!"

ANNA'S MOTHER: "Okay, when I was really little, ya know? About your age. I played with my sister and she's older than me, ya know?"

ANNA: "Yes!

ANNA'S MOTHER: "Well, my mother said, 'Don't you go near that vase.'"

ANNA: "Yes, don't do that!"

If we look at the three children, Mateo, Lucy, and Anna, we can see that their development, like all humans, involves guided interactions between and among their parents/guardians, family, and family's community. That is, as children grow, the

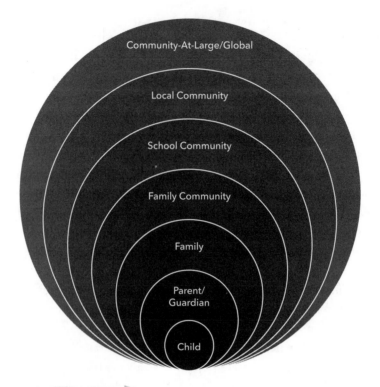

Figure 2.1: Circles of Interactions

activities they engage in occur through the supports they receive from those who care for them. Further, these supports and contacts with others grow as do their ever-expanding understanding of the world around them (Rogoff, 1990; 2003). As they become school age, their circles of interactions expand to include their school community and all who are part of it (e.g., their teachers, peers, support staff, administrators, cafeteria workers, office staff), continue to expand outward to the local community in which they are being reared, and further to the larger and even global community in which they participate (Zacarian and Silverstone, 2015). Figure 2.1, adapted from Zacarian and Silverstone, 2015; Zacarian, 2017, illustrates the ever-expanding circles of interactions that occur during a child's development.

Rogoff (1990) calls the interactive experiences children engage in, such as the bedtime rituals we described for Mateo, Lucy, and Anna, an "apprenticeship that occurs through guided participation in social activity with companions who support and stretch children's understanding of and skill in using the tools of culture" (p. 1). She also highlights a significant element in this growth—that of the active participation of the child in their own development.

Consider the examples of Mateo, Lucy, and Anna. Describe the supports each child is given to participate actively in the interactions we have described.

1. What are one to two supports that Mateo's family used to help him participate actively in interactions?

    _____

    _____

    _____

    _____

2. What are one to two supports that Lucy's grandmother used to help her participate actively in interactions?

    _____

    _____

    _____

3. What are one to two supports that Anna's parents used to help her participate actively in interactions?

    _____

    _____

    _____

A second and important characteristic of all human development is that we are raised according to the cultural norms and expectations of the groups in which we are reared. Rogoff (2003) highlights the significance of this by explaining some key distinctions between groups. For example, where many U.S. middle-class families might not regard children under the age of 14 as being capable caregivers, many from other cultures do, such as an eight-year-old from Guatemala who cares for her young cousin (Rogoff, 2003). Another example Rogoff highlights is the use of tools, such as machetes, by very young children in the Ituri Forest of the Democratic Republic of Congo. They use this tool at a very young age to cut fruit. This cultural way of being and acting differs greatly from the tools used by young children being reared in the U.S. In the U.S., young children's tools are mostly made out of light plastic or wood without any rough edges to be sure that sharp objects are kept far away from them for fear that they might hurt themselves or others (Rogoff, 2003). While these two examples might not reflect the same types of experiences that all of us are familiar with, the point is that our culture contributes to our understanding of the world around us and our place in it. Our three examples highlight some of the cultural differences among children who are the same age. Mateo's family, for example, is rearing him to use the type of language and literacy that they believe is important for his future.

THE INFLUENCE OF POSITIVE AND CONSTRAINING OPPORTUNITIES ON IDENTITY

Regardless of children's many differences, two of the common critical elements that are present in each child's development is that they are unconditionally loved and valued. Another, and this cannot be underscored enough, is that their individual families possess many strengths and assets. While we have not described these in any detail for the three children, we may find ourselves making some assumptions about each of them that perceives them as missing something.

We might think, for example, that Mateo is not fluent in English, that Lucy does not live with her parents, and/or that Anna is experiencing tremendous turmoil as a homeless child. In other words, we might view each as having something that is "broken" or "missing" and that needs remedying (Ginsberg, 2015). All too often, this deficit-based view forces us to *look at* what we perceive as wrong or missing or deficient instead of *looking for* what is already there; that is, the strengths and qualities that all humans possess (Zacarian, Alvarez-Ortiz, and Haynes, 2018). Our earlier example of Lynn Pelkey shows us what can happen when we have this perspective. She describes what she often overheard from her teachers: a deficit-based view of her capacities and skills. This negatively impacted her perceptions of herself and her identity. What science has shown is that these types of deficit-based perceptions and assumptions can and often do lead to poor outcomes (Park, Groth, Bradley, and Rorer, 2018).

USING STRENGTHS-BASED CULTURALLY RESPONSIVE PRACTICES

There is a good deal of research that points to the urgency for us to see *and* look for the strengths and assets that all students and families possess. These should lead us to seek the type of culturally responsive strengths-based practices that acknowledge, value, and view our students as competent and reflect the qualities we identify back to them so that they may acknowledge and see these in themselves. Let's have a look at what we mean by the critical importance of acknowledging and valuing and seeing students' and families' competencies.

Scholars and researchers in equity, linguistics, and diversity—González, Moll, and Amanti (2005); González (2005); and González, Moll, Tenery, Rivera, Rendon, Gonzales & Amanti (2005)—are renowned for their research and findings about the depth of knowledge and assets that all families possess. Drawing from earlier research on the importance of valuing the competencies of families, Moll, Amanti, Neff, and González (1992) coined the term *funds of knowledge* to describe the many strengths and assets that all people possess and, more importantly, how important it is for educators to honor, acknowledge, and value these. They researched families with limited prior schooling who were living on the border region between Mexico and the United States. While many might assume that students' parents were unable to support their children's studies because of their limited prior schooling, they found that the families possessed a myriad of skills, talents, and knowledge that related to their well-being, home life, and work. They found that families naturally tended to pass these understandings and practices (these funds of knowledge) on to their children. Most importantly, they contributed to the practice of teaching by declaring the importance of honoring and valuing the strengths of all families and that these connections can and do have a positive outcome on our students.

Additionally, the principles of *positive psychology* (Maslow, 1999; Morris & Maisto, 2002) and a *growth mindset* (Dweck, 2006) ask us to see the possibilities that can be realized when we focus on the inherent strengths of individuals and communities and when we demonstrate our belief in the accomplishments of others. The type of unconditional acceptance of this human trait of positivity asks that we find the strengths and capacities in each of our students. It is not that we ignore what is occurring in their lives, such as Anna being homeless and her parents searching for more stable housing. It is that culturally responsive practices require that we place as much attention and intention on identifying and focusing on students' and families' strengths and assets as we do on what is happening in their lives. One of the most important practices for considering the type of unconditional acceptance that we are referring to is how we can support our students to see their own and their peers' strengths and competencies and engage in interactions that meaningfully and precisely demonstrate these proactively empowering and positive beliefs.

An example of what we mean is sociologist Pedro Noguera's writings on the effect of racial identity on schooling (2002). Drawing from a personal example, he recounts how well his eldest son, Joaquín, performed in school and as an athlete and a musician. When Joaquín reached tenth grade, however, his grades dramatically dropped as did his attitude about school. Noguera uses this personal example to explain the influences that surrounded his son, including the reality that those who Joaquín had close personal ties and connections to in his mostly poor urban neighborhood were dropping out of school. Noguera understood the actions of his son, having experienced them himself as a Black adolescent, and understood how his son "felt he had to present himself when he was out in the streets and in school," figuring out his identity as a young Black man.

Noguera highlights research he did that demonstrated two critical aspects for understanding differences as they relate to culturally responsive practices.

1. The more interactions we have with other groups of people, the more likely we are to understand and appreciate them.
2. The less contact we have with others, the less understanding we might have about what we perceive as our differences and the wider the gulf becomes as the groups remain separated (2002).

His research and findings affirm what we are calling for: the urgent necessity for culturally responsive practices where:

- students are essential members of and not isolated from their peers;
- they learn to be empathetic toward their peers and others;
- the four essential conditions of a culture of caring are ever present; and
- the use of sociocultural consciousness about ourselves and others is omnipresent.

SUPPORTING STUDENTS' POSITIVE IDENTITY DEVELOPMENT AS A COLLECTIVE

Our interactive approach toward understanding identity as socially and interactionally constructed requires that we collaborate with students and their families and our colleagues and others with whom we work so that our culturally responsive practices are what educational scholars Fullan and Hargreaves (2012) call a "collective accomplishment and responsibility." The ideals of the type of collaboration we are calling for sees the success of all students as everyone's mission. Unlike the experience of Lawrence-Lightfoot and Pelky, it is also a mission where the language that we use to interact about, with, and on behalf of our students reflects a clear drive toward collective equity—one in which groups of students from underrepresented and dominant groups are all high achieving and learn how to embrace and value each other using culturally responsive practices that transcend across students, families, school communities, and more.

Educational scholars Elizabeth Cohen and Rachel Lotan have contributed greatly to our understanding of students from diverse experiences who perceive themselves and/or others to be of high and low status (Cohen & Lotan, 2014; Lotan, 2006). They looked closely at the concept of equity as it related to when students learned and worked together. One of the key elements of their research contributions is the significance of teachers' role in supporting students to care about themselves and others by taking time to identify, recognize, and value the strengths and capacities that all students bring. We will discuss this in more detail in our succeeding chapters.

It would be impossible for us to write this chapter without recognizing and acknowledging the epic numbers of students experiencing trauma, violence, and chronic stress, as well as the urgency for our understanding of the type of interactions and actions that we must take to support the inherent strengths and capacities of this group. According to the National Survey of Children's Health (2011/2012), more than half of the nation's children have or are experiencing one or more significant forms of childhood adversity (National Survey of Children's Health, 2011/2012):

- physical, sexual, or verbal abuse;
- physical and emotional neglect;
- a parent who is an alcoholic (or addicted to other drugs);
- witnessing domestic abuse;
- a family member in jail;
- loss of a parent to death or abandonment, including abandonment by parental divorce; and
- mental illness or a depressed or suicidal person in the home.

While all too many of us may view such students as too traumatized to succeed or feel hopeless in our capacity to support their success, there are large and growing bodies of research that support the urgency for using an asset-based approach. We have only to look to the fields of psychotherapy and positive psychology (Seligman, Rashid & Parks, 2006), psychology (Dweck, Walton and Cohen, 2014, Dweck 2006), positive youth development (Floyd & McKenna, 2003; Lerner et al, 2005), and educational research in diversity and equity (Biswas-Dienera, Kashdan & Gurpal, 2011; González, Moll & Amanti, 2006; Steele, 2010) to see the positive possibilities of it.

It is not that we are dismissing or ignoring what is happening in the lives of the epic numbers experiencing these phenomena. It is that we are putting as much, if not more, emphasis on what is positive and possible in their lives when we support them in identifying the many strengths and capacities they possess and drawing from these strengths routinely in their lives. Dr. Jeff Duncan-Andrade, a professor at San Francisco State University and founder of and board chair at the Roses in Concrete Community School in Oakland (which we will feature in a later chapter), discussed the meaning of the name of the school he founded and the importance of returning to Maslow's Hierarchy of Needs in working with students experiencing adversity. He said, "The concrete is real and it's multilayered and it's toxic. . . . If schools are not aware of the concrete and that students are showing up with damaged petals, then we can't see those roses" (KQED news article, 2018). Duncan-Andrade suggests that, although educators have known about Maslow's Hierarchy of Needs for decades, this work must be at the center of everything we do.

APPLYING MASLOW'S THEORY

Maslow's original hierarchy of a five-stage model (1987) stated that people are motivated to achieve certain needs and that some take precedence over others. Our most basic need is for physical survival, and this will be the first thing that motivates our behavior. Once that level is fulfilled, the next level up is what motivates us, and so on. The Hierarchy of Needs is explained, as follows.

1. **Physiological needs:** These are biological requirements for human survival, e.g., air, food, drink, shelter, clothing, warmth, sleep. If these needs are not satisfied, the human body cannot function optimally. Maslow considered physiological needs the most important as all the other needs become secondary until these needs are met.
2. **Safety needs:** These include protection from elements, security, order, law, stability, and freedom from fear.
3. **Love and belongingness needs:** After physiological and safety needs have been fulfilled, the third level of human needs is social and involves feelings of belongingness. The need for interpersonal relationships motivates behavior. Examples include friendship, intimacy, trust, acceptance, receiving and giving affection, love, affiliating, and being part of a group (family, friends, work).
4. **Esteem needs:** Maslow classified these into two categories: esteem for oneself (dignity, achievement, mastery, independence) and the desire for reputation or respect from others (status, prestige). Maslow indicated that the need for respect or reputation is most important for children and adolescents and precedes real self-esteem or dignity.
5. **Self-actualization needs:** These include realizing personal potential, self-fulfillment, seeking personal growth, peak experiences, and a desire "to become everything one is capable of becoming" (Maslow, 1987, p. 64).

Duncan-Andrade applies Maslow's work in school settings by aligning the use of the 3Rs in education alongside self-actualization: relationships, relevance, and responsibility. In terms of relationships, Duncan-Andrade, who also teaches at the Roses in Concrete Community School, believes that it is essential students believe he cares about them on that basic level before they will be willing to learn from him. He states, "At the end of the day, effective teaching depends most heavily on one thing: deep and caring relationships." In his essay, Duncan-Andrade suggests that, "The adage 'Students don't care what you know until they know that you care' is supported by numerous studies of effective educators" (Duncan-Andrade, 2018).

The urgent need for caring about and for our students is also supported by many in therapeutic fields who have shown, over the course of decades, the urgency for moving from a deficit-based to an asset-based lens. According to experts in behavioral health, Hertel and Johnson (2013), for example, one of the most important means that teachers have for supporting children who are faced with unpredictable, illogical, disorganized, inconsistent, and volatile home lives is to reconsider "how we teach social, emotional, and academic learning" (Hertel and Johnson, 2013, pp. 29–32). They propose that we consider the usage of six principles in all we do to support students' "social, emotional, and academic learning":

1. Always empower and never disempower.
2. Provide unconditional positive regard.
3. Maintain high expectations.
4. Check assumptions, observe, and question.
5. Be a relationship coach.
6. Provide opportunities for meaningful participation. (p. 31–32)

While we will discuss this in further detail in succeeding chapters, it is important to note that they and others advocate, as we are doing, that we acknowledge the complex nature of adverse childhood experiences *and* create routine conditions in all we do in our schools to support students to care for themselves and others in positive ways so that they may succeed in school and in their lives. Sadly, Duncan-Andrade states that schools are not equipping teachers to handle this type of health crisis. He punctuated his point, stating, "The symptoms [of adversity] are more complex than what they're seeing in the military. The best I see in schools is a one-off training on trauma, and now you're trauma-informed and go help those kids" (Schwartz, 2018). His point is well taken. To support students' positive identity development, we must create conditions that provide what behavioral analyst Ladona Wiebler describes as "consistency, predictability, structure, and the opportunity to develop caring relationships" (Wiebler, 2013, p. 40). As we will see in our succeeding chapter, we believe that classrooms are ideal places for students to learn, internalize, and use the social and emotional communication skills they need to learn and work together so that they each feel safe, are members of their classroom and school communities, and feel valued, competent, and socially responsible for others.

To do this, Duncan-Andrade recommends we connect the dots between Maslow's framework and the latest research on inequality with the primary human needs consistently under attack for many students of color. He suggests we need to be willing to confront the harsh realities of social inequalities with our pedagogy and the routines and practices that we do every day, so that students can begin to have hope. Duncan-Andrade recommends that hope—real hope and not false hope—can be a way to combat ACEs and complex post-traumatic stress disorder. "Hope is the best indicator for the degree to which kids will successfully navigate toxic stress, and the degree to which kids are less likely to engage in self-harming behavior," Duncan-Andrade suggested in a MindShift interview (Schwartz, 2018).

1. How do you currently apply or use Maslow's Hierarchy of Needs in your classroom? How do you see yourself applying this work after reading Duncan-Andrade's work?

_____

_____

_____

2. How can you incorporate and model hope—real hope—in your own classroom?

_____

_____

_____

In our next chapter, we will begin to explore some of the tools of a culturally responsive approach to education, where students' personal, cultural, and social identities are central to the curriculum that is chosen and the approaches that we use to teach are meaningfully socially connected around issues of social justice and equity.

3

Building a Balanced Approach
to Culturally Responsive Teaching

WHEN STEPHEN WANG took his state's annual tenth-grade mathematics exam, he believed his answers were forthright and would fulfill the requirements needed to graduate high school. When his mathematics scores were revealed many months later, however, they were well below the threshold. His low scores meant that he would have to retake the test and, hopefully, raise his score by the needed 20 points. Discouraged, he wondered if he would ever pass the test and began debating with himself whether it would make more sense for him to drop out of school entirely. Simultaneously, as he was filled with these disparaging thoughts, a team of educators including his school's guidance counselor, math teacher, and Title 1 support staff met to review his results. They noted that Stephen had skipped a lot of the math problems and received no credit for them. They also saw that his responses to the questions that he had answered were mostly correct.

With this information, the team eagerly met with Stephen to learn about his rationale for leaving blank responses to so many problems. His math teacher began the conversation. She said, "Stephen, you answered so many problems successfully, which is great. However, you left many blank. Why didn't you respond to each question?" Stephen shared that he only answered the problems for which he was sure of the answers. He used expressions such as "That would make me look bad" and "Making mistakes is not a good thing to do" in reference to his choice of skipping them. Each of his responses reflected what was important to him as a learner. They also helped the team understand that Stephen did not know about or had not internalized and committed himself to practicing the efficacy of making a strategic guess. Rather, he thought that he had done the right thing by skipping over the problems for which he was even slightly unsure of the answers. Rather than require him to take an entire course review to prepare him for the retest, his math teacher recommended an alternative plan.

She recommended meeting with Stephen twice a week to support his learning how to use a guessing technique that would help him to recognize the types of math problems that would be on the state exam. She also recommended that to do this, she would tailor the math tutorials around his interests. For example, when she found out that Stephen was passionate about climate change and had been thinking about attending college to major in environmental studies, she said she would create math problems that were based on that topic. With his full agreement, she supported him to see the usage of guessing techniques as a positive reflection of his mathematics knowledge and identity as opposed to his earlier perception of seeing guessing as a sign of weakness. In addition, she showed him a variety of techniques that mathematicians use, including making a strategic and conditional guess, so that he could see the value of using these practices, too. After three months of tutorials on this topic, Stephen took the retest exam, passed it, and graduated from high school on time with his peers.

If we met with his math teacher about the tutorial experiences that she had with Stephen, she would tell us that their interactions helped her to see how important it is for us to use a teaching approach that takes into account our students' personal, social, and cultural identities in all of the choices we make and the approaches we use.

In this chapter, we examine a culturally responsive educational approach where:

- the *who* and *what* we teach involves a matched balanced approach and
- the approaches we use to teach must be meaningfully socially connected around issues of social justice and equity.

THE WHO AND WHAT WE TEACH INVOLVES USING A MATCHED BALANCED APPROACH

In our book, we have used the word *balanced* to describe the actions that we must take to support a culturally responsive classroom. A common image that is often used to describe the word *balance* is a scale with two pans on either side that are filled with the same or an equal amount of weights. The type of scale we are referring to when we use the word *balance* is one that has no fixed state of permanence. Rather, our image of it relates to what we do to maintain a sense of balance or equilibrium by continuously adjusting ourselves to the dynamic changes in our student

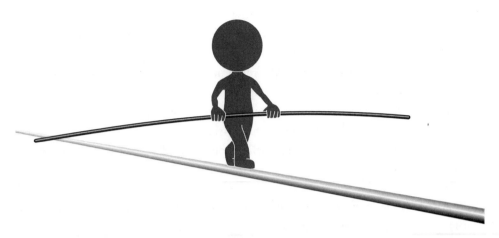

Figure 3.1: A Balanced Approach

and family populations, the curriculum we teach, and society itself. We use Figure 3.1 to describe the type of movement that we believe educators must continuously make to achieve that ever-changing state of a balanced approach.

While some of us might view walking a tight rope as a dangerous undertaking, let's assuage that fear by saying that the rope sits just a few inches off of the ground and that we can easily slip off and back on the rope. What is critical for our using this figurative and imaginative way of thinking is that our balance is dependent on the actions that *we* take rather than what our curriculum somehow magically does or will do or that our ever-changing students do or will do to make education work. Let's look more deeply at the concept of who we teach and then what we teach to look more closely at this creative image.

WHO WE TEACH

Who we teach has a good deal to do with the principles and practices we enact. Let's say, for example, that two new students enroll in Stephen's science class in March (well into the academic year) for their first exposure to geology. One of the students emigrated from Honduras, is a beginning learner of English, and has not been exposed to an American public school. The other moved from a neighboring state. Our science teacher is not sure that either of the new students has had any education in the unit of study that she is teaching in geology. She begins thinking about the steps that she should take to make learning meaningful and purposeful. She also wants, as many teachers do, to ensure that the two new students as well as all of her students feel that they are valued contributing members in her science class; and that their work together is meaningful as well as responsive in terms of their caring for and about each other. In Chapter 2, we introduced the importance of what Duncan-Andrade (2019) refers to as the three Rs: relationships, relevance, and responsibility. A crucial element of creating these conditions is to learn as much as we can about who our students are so that we can build instructional programming that will match their personal, cultural, social, and world experiences and interests as well as their prior academic experiences. With this in mind, let's engage in a reflection activity about the steps you believe the science teacher will take.

Describe two to three steps you think the science teacher should take to build an instructional program that is based on her students' backgrounds. _____

_____

_____

_____

As educators, we have control over our own actions. So, being the teacher we believe this science teacher and most are, let's make her actions work to their best advantage so that students, such as Stephen and his two new classmates, can learn successfully. To do this, let's look more closely at what we mean by using a balanced approach in a culturally responsive classroom by going back to Stephen, our focal student in this chapter, and discussing who he is as a person.

Let's add some additional details about Stephen to help us in understanding the concept of a balanced approach. Stephen was born in Newark, New Jersey. His parents emigrated from Taiwan before Stephen was conceived. While Stephen has traveled to Taiwan to visit his maternal and paternal grandparents, his usage of oral Mandarin is, at best, at the early-intermediate stage, where he can make his needs known and carry on a basic conversation with his parents and grandparents. Stephen is not literate in Mandarin and has never received a language assistance program in Mandarin or English. As a native speaker of English, he has learned alongside his English-speaking peers in mainstream classrooms. However, his family engages in many of the cultural heritage practices found in their home country. These include that it is important not to lose face with others and to be seen as harmonious with others (Chen, 2000). An example of this is Stephen's mother, a master seamstress. Stephen accompanied her to JOANN Fabrics, where she purchased some goods to repair a customer's dress. When the salesperson tried to sell his mother alternative materials, she politely declined by saying "You the expert, but I am okay." Indeed, this polite discourse is emblematic of the type of interactions Stephen's mother, father, and siblings have with others. They are always polite, never offensive, and make sure they do not say anything that would embarrass themselves in front of others.

1. How do or don't our descriptions of Stephen's family relate to his skipping some of the problems on the state's mathematics exam and the interactions he had with the team of his school's mathematics teacher, guidance counselor, and Title 1 teacher?

   _____

   _____

2. Describe two to three ways that Stephen's teacher adapted her instruction to Stephen's interests and learning needs.

   _____

   _____

3. When you learned that Stephen is Chinese-American, what surprised you about him? What didn't surprise you and why?

   _____

   _____

   _____

4. How are Stephen's family's cultural practices the same or different from the practices your family engages in?

   _____

   _____

   _____

INDIVIDUALIST AND COLLECTIVIST CULTURAL PRACTICES

It is essential that we consider the differences among our students' home communities, particularly students whose families represent U.S.-dominant culture in which independence and competition are highly valued norms, as well as students whose families from underrepresented cultures lean toward a collectivist cultural system where group harmony and interpersonal relationships are highly coveted norms (Hofstede, 2001; Hofstede & Hofstede, 2005; DeCapua & Marshall, 2010; Tyler et al, 2008). Although it is impossible to express these in absolutes, as so many students represent hybrid experiences, the differences between students from individualistic and collectivistic cultural beliefs are critical to consider, particularly because we may lean toward using approaches that are a mismatch for students from groups other than our own (Tyler et al, 2008). In Chapter 1, we shared demographic information about most U.S. educators—that they are White and middle class. As such, the majority of educators lean toward a preference for an individualistic approach because it is a match with their dominant cultural frame of reference. And, the U.S. dominant culture is not the only country that places a high value on individualism; so do Western Europeans, Australians, and Canadians (Rothstein-Fish and Trumbull, 2008). People from this culture value "individual responsibility for self, independence, self-reliance, self-expression, self-esteem, and task over process" (p. 9). Two of the most prominent distinctions between individualist and collectivist cultural educational practices are that the: (1) former lean toward preferring a quiet classroom, limited student interactions, and tasks and activities that are done independently, and (2) latter favor interdependence and interconnectedness where students' interactions and relationships are of high value (American Psychological Association, 2003; Tyler et al, 2008). While each ethnically diverse group has their own cultural way of being and acting, the common thread of collectivism is evident across all (Tyler et al, 2008).

An important element to add to our discussion about collectivism is its foundations in the importance of relationships. In school settings, this includes the critical importance of relationships between students and their teachers. Educational researcher John Hattie (2008) conducted a meta-analysis of the 138 influential factors affecting student achievement. Teacher–student relationships and teacher feedback ranked among the top 8%. This finding resonates with the research on students from collectivist cultures. It also points to the importance of our building strong relationships with our students from the start and harkens back to the points that Duncan-Andrade (2019) discusses as it relates to the urgency for building relationships, relevance, and responsibility from the get-go. Here are some strategies for engaging in these three Rs with students from the start.

STRATEGIES FOR CO-CREATING A CLASSROOM DESIGN AND BUILDING RELATIONSHIPS FROM THE START

In general terms, the first person that is critical in order for students to feel safety, security, and belonging in their classroom community is their teacher. Whether we are referring to students in grades preK–16, it is essential for us to take steps that support students in feeling the sense of safety we discussed in Chapter 2 regarding Maslow's Hierarchy of Needs. Some practical strategies for this are to ensure that we genuinely welcome students into our classrooms, regardless of when they enroll during the school year, and support them to feel that they are true members of our communities. Setting up the physical environment so that it feels like a student's home away from home is a

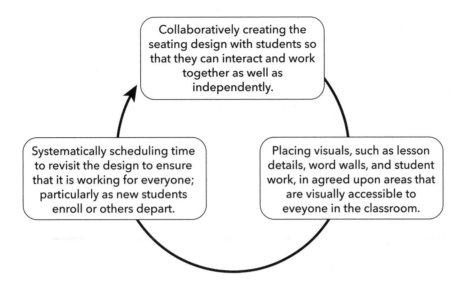

Figure 3.2: Co-creating the Classroom Design

helpful way of thinking. A means for doing this is to consider what we can do to cooperatively create our classroom design with students so that they have an important role to play in their own learning and have a voice and choice around what works best for them. Some strategies for doing this are seen in Figure 3.2.

One reason for supporting the urgency for thinking responsibly about our classroom design is the positive effect it can have on students who might perceive themselves to be in a racial, economic, cultural, linguistic, ethnic, or gender group that is perceived negatively (Steele, 2010). For example, let's say that the science teacher's new student from Honduras does not feel safe coming to a new country, new city, new home, and new school, especially one that communicates in a language he is not yet familiar with. In addition, he has also heard that Americans don't like immigrants, particularly those from his country, and he fears for his own safety. Drawing from Duncan-Andrade's points about Maslow's Hierarchy of Needs, it is critical that we design a classroom environment in which he will feel safe first followed by a sense of belonging to his new classroom, school, and local community. To do this, we must work with everyone in our classroom so that it is more than just a teacher effort but also a community effort. An example of this type of effort is our science teacher. She is accustomed to students moving into her school district during the school year and has taken steps to proactively prepare herself and her existing students for a new arrival. Adapting strategies from Keith Maletta, a teacher from North Carolina (Zacarian and Silverstone, 2015), she asks students to complete the following questions in Figure 3.3 on their first day of class:

Figure 3.3: Activities Science Teacher Asks

- Activities that you are involved with at our school, were involved with at your last school, or would like to be involved with.
- Activities you like to do at home.
- Activities you participate in and/or work you do outside of school
- Rate your interest in learning science from one to five, five being the strongest.
- Rate your interest as a reader (especially reading about science!) from one to five.
- Rate yourself as a communicator from one to five.
- Rate yourself as a lab partner from one to five.
- Rate your ability to get along with other from one to five.

The intent of this strategy is to learn about her students' interests and the activities they participate or would like to participate in both in and out of school. Her goal is to support students to become involved with others in a variety of communities (classroom, school, after-school clubs, sport teams, local community). She also draws from this information throughout the school year in a variety of ways. For example, two questions ask students to rate themselves as a lab partner and their ability to get along with others. Her intent in asking these is to support pair and group assignments that are likely to work well. She often pairs students who rate themselves differently on the scale as she finds that these groupings tend to work best in her class. She also pairs a new student with peers who rate themselves highly in working with a partner and getting along with others to support a helpful entrée. Also, she re-administers the same activity at the mid-point each semester to make adjustments in grouping assignments and support student involvement with others.

An additional strategy some teachers use to learn about their students is to ask each student the following open-ended question: *What do I wish my teacher knew about me?* (Zacarian, Alvarez-Ortiz, & Haynes, 2018). While this open-ended question is often applied to young learners, it can easily be used with students at all grade levels. Here are some examples of the types of responses our science teacher received:

"I like science, but I don't want anyone to know I do."

"I hate science. It's too hard and there's too much to learn and I feel dumb in science."

"I don't know what geology is."

The beauty of an open-ended question such as this is that it can lead to a dialogue where we can learn about our students and their personal, social, cultural, academic, and world experiences and connect these with our instruction to build meaningfully interconnected learning experiences.

Elena Aguilar (2012) provides a list of questions to ask at the start of a school year or as new students enroll.

- Tell me about a teacher you really liked and what they did that you appreciated.
- Tell me about a teacher you felt wasn't effective and why.
- What do you think makes a "good" teacher?
- Describe the most interesting activity you ever did in school.
- Describe the most challenging class or unit of study.
- How do you like to get feedback?
- If I notice that you're not following one of our classroom agreements, how would you like me to let you know?
- On a scale of 1–5, how much do you like reading? (1: not at all, 2: sort of/ sometimes, 3: most of the time, 4: I like reading, 5: I LOVE reading)
- On a scale of 1–5, how would you rate your reading skills? (1: I'm a terrible reader, 2: I'm not a very good reader, 3: I'm an OK reader, 4: I'm a good reader, 5: I'm a really, really good reader)
- What did you read last year in school or outside of school?
- Who do you know who likes to read?
- Outside of school, who do you think believes in you and supports you most?
- Who do you want me to tell when you do really well in school?
- Tell me about something that's been hard for you in your life.
- Tell me about something you feel proud of.
- Tell me about something you love doing that has nothing to do with school.
- What's your favorite thing to do on the weekend?
- If you could have three wishes, what would they be?
- What would you like to know about me?
- What else can you tell me that would help me be a better teacher for you?

Another activity that teachers can use, particularly at the beginning of the school year, is to have students share the linguistic and cultural history associated with their names. For example, Soto has her students discuss the following questions with a partner: 1) What is the story of your name? 2) What cultural or linguistic history does it carry? (Soto & Hetzel, 2009). Teachers may also have students interview their parents and/or family members about their names. This activity is based on the "My Name, My Identity" Campaign: A Declaration of Self, started by the Santa Clara County Office of Education in California. The "My Name, My Identity" website and campaign asserts that, "By pronouncing students' names correctly, you can foster a sense of belonging and build positive relationships in the classroom, which are crucial for healthy social, psychological, and educational outcomes" (https://www.mynamemyidentity.org). By going to the website, educators will find additional "getting to know our names" resources and can take the pledge to respect students' names.

It's helpful to pick and choose questions that we envision will help support our students' success in school. You may wish to include all or some of these at different intervals during the school year.

APPLYING CULTURALLY RESPONSIVE PRACTICES TO PEER–PEER LEARNING

Many educators use cooperative learning methods in their work with students, believing it can be a profoundly effective approach. Educational scholars Elizabeth Cohen and Rachel Lotan have contributed greatly to our understanding of this approach as it applies to students from diverse experiences who perceive themselves and/or others to be of high and low status (Cohen & Lotan, 2014; Lotan, 2006). The scholars looked closely at the concept of equity in collaborative group settings and intentionally creating tasks and activities that would have a positive impact on the ways that students learned and worked together. One of the key elements of their research was how teachers could support interactions that would help everyone to feel safe, a sense of belonging, valued, competent, and socially responsible for themselves and their peers. One of their findings is the importance of recognizing the different skills and talents that all students bring. They found that two conditions must be present to better ensure that there is a positive influence on a group's collective work and on an individual's academic and social growth.

The first condition is that educators understand and believe that all students and families possess great intelligence, talents, and capacities. This involves our taking time to identify the various strengths and talents of our students by keenly observing what they do and say, asking them questions to learn about who they are as individuals and their interests and desires, and, whenever possible, meeting with their families to further tap into the possibilities of strengths and capacities. The second condition that they found must be present is our taking time to acknowledge and validate each of the strengths that we identify so that our students see these in themselves and others. What is key for this to occur is our taking time to create tasks that allow students to demonstrate their talents and skills. While we will discuss this in more detail in succeeding chapters, the notion of equity cannot be underscored enough.

An example of what we mean is an experience that one of our author's teams had in an upper-grade elementary classroom where students were asked to solve a problem set involving multiplying fractions. One small group consisted of four monolingual speakers of American English, a recent arrival from Japan at the very beginning stage of learning English, and a Japanese-English translator. While the small group was working together, the teacher observed them carefully. She observed that the translator didn't speak to the student and, yet, each student was writing on a piece of paper. When the group raised their hands in unison to let their teacher know that they had solved the problem set, she came to the group and asked, "What strategies did you use to solve the problem?" Expecting to hear an assortment of answers, they all pointed to the recent arrival and explained that he helped them to draw it out on paper. A few weeks later, with the help of the translator, the student shared with his small group that he felt alone and isolated and that his math class with them was the only time he felt that he was as popular and well liked as he had been in Japan. After he said this, each member acknowledged how helpful his drawings were in making mathematics easier to learn. One student said, "I would have failed without you!"

When setting up equitable environments for peer–peer learning, it is essential to integrate norms and procedures that encourage interdependence, as well as design group-worthy tasks. Peer–peer learning is often not natural for most students and must be explicitly taught, modeled, and practiced often. As teacher and curriculum coordinator, Heather Wolpert-Gawron (2019) shared in an Edutopia infographic, "If students don't collaborate well, that's your clue to do it more often, not less. But structure it. Teach them how to create norms, find consensus, and move on after a disagreement." Soto explains peer-peer learning as being comfortable and engaging for students, as it represents a "familia," or a family unit, in the classroom setting. Since many students of color come from more communal and less independently oriented cultural orientations, peer–peer learning can encourage and should require active participation, as well as allow student voices and academic identities to emerge. The following is a sample set of norms and procedures that an English teacher, Danny Magana, from South El Monte High School in Southern California and Soto (2015) have outlined in the article *Creating Classroom Buzz*. Students in Magana's ninth-grade classroom co-developed the following group norms during their reciprocal reading conversations, which were based on the four reciprocal teaching roles: summarizer, questioner, connector, and predictor. Magana elicited students' opinions by asking them what they thought would assist a group with running smoothly in the classroom setting. Students suggested:

- Everybody in the group contributes equally.
- Be respectful of group members and their opinions.
- Stay focused on the task and your own group.
- Pay attention to what other people need. It's not about you, it's about the group.
- No one is done until everyone is done.

Similarly, Lotan (2003) in her article, *Group Worthy Tasks*, suggests that there are five design features essential in creating "group-worthy" tasks. The five design features include:

- Open-ended tasks—grappling with real-life uncertainties and ambiguities. Tasks can include designing an experiment, building a model, interpreting an important historical document, explicating a poem, solving an authentic mathematical problem, or reconciling different points of view in potentially divisive debate.
- Multiple ways to show competence—this is where students get to demonstrate their creativity! They can make contributions to the group effort by using various talents, intellectual competencies, and diverse repertoires of problem-solving strategies. This can include building structures, creating murals, composing and performing songs, acting in plays, and designing inventions.
- Significant content—students should not complete simple tasks in groups. Instead, they need to work on tasks where they need each other to be successful. They need to interact, discuss, and clarify thoughts that are connected to a big idea, essential question, or disciplinary concept.
- Interdependence and individual accountability—many of us grew up not enjoying group work because it was not productive or equitable. Perhaps many of us completed all of the tasks for the group. Instead, teachers must model how to arrive at a group consensus, while also holding each student accountable for mastering concepts. This can be done by allotting points for both individual and group tasks and/or using a rubric that holds students accountable for interdependent and individual contributions.
- Clear evaluation criteria—providing specific criteria as to what makes an exemplary group product, as well as providing models of exemplary work, improves interactions amongst group members.

These five design features, as well as setting group norms, reminds educators that peer–peer learning must be carefully and intentionally planned to be effective and productive. Teachers who teach the same grade level or content area can spend time planning group-worthy tasks during their collaboration time so that they can support each other throughout the process.

WHAT WE TEACH

Regardless of the ages of the students that we teach (i.e., from young children to adult), we want all students to be active, participatory, and even excited about the subject matter. Our quest to do this is of keen interest to those of us engaged in advancing student achievement as well as experts in the fields of science, technology, and mathematics who have brought to light the nation's critical shortage of professionals in these respective fields (National Academies of Sciences, Engineering, and Medicine, 2017; Adams and Hamm, 2014). A challenge for all educators is making the curriculum come alive for our students in ways that will pique and even compel their interest to learn. Let's say, for example, that we observe Stephen's science class, where he is learning some of the principle theories of geology, including tectonic plates. His course text (more than 500 pages!) is loaded with page after page of bolded vocabulary words such as *lithosphere, exosphere, thermosphere, mesosphere, stratosphere, troposphere, crust, upper mantle, mantle, outer core,* and *inner core.* Further, the type of language used in the text is very dense and geology specific. Here is an example of a typical sentence from the type of course text we are referring to:

Example 1: Subject-specific Text

The asthenosphere is below the lithosphere. It is located in a deeper part of the upper mantle.

The constant presence of new vocabulary and sophisticated science-specific language throughout this type of course text makes learning challenging for many students, including Stephen. It is difficult to meaningfully comprehend subject-matter concepts *and* sustain an interest in learning.

Such challenges require that we use a balanced approach to culturally responsive practices by making sure that we continuously balance what we do to teach subject matters in ways that support student learning. The type of balancing actions we are referring to must take into account four distinct elements of the learning process. Namely, the *what* we teach must be a match to our students' sociocultural, linguistic, academic, and thinking experiences and bodies of knowledge. These four elements, listed in Figure 3.4, form what we know as *what we do* to support students to learn by building connections with the strengths and assets of the knowledge they already possess.

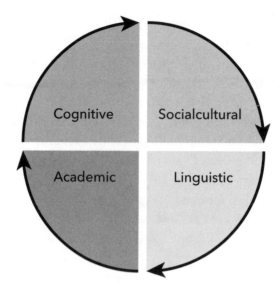

Figure 3.4: The Learning Process Involves Four Elements *(Adapted from Zacarian, 2013)*

Each of these interdependent elements must be continuously present to build successful culturally responsive practices. While we introduced the concept of these four elements in our first chapter, let's look at how they relate to what we teach to build a balanced culturally responsive practice.

1. **Learning is a sociocultural process.** One of the most critical elements in choosing what we teach is ensuring that it connects to our students' lives, preferences, and interests in meaningful and purposeful ways. A purchased course text, such as Stephen's science textbook, or instructional materials created by a school or district, will never spark the interests and desires of all of our students. One of our biggest reasons for stating this with confidence is that they were not written for our particular students or their unique interests. Rather, curriculum writing is generally based on a target goal or objective of what its authors expect students to learn and be able to do as a demonstration of their learning accomplishments. Further, it is usually based on a standard from the school, district, or state. Thus, the *what* we teach requires that we take the steps needed to ensure the curriculum connects meaningfully to or matches with our students' personal, social, cultural, and world experiences, preferences, and interests. While we will discuss how we can do this later in this chapter, let's look at one example of a sociocultural match between the content being taught and a student's personal, social, cultural, and world experiences.

Example of the Sociocultural Element in Practice

Stephen, our tenth-grade focal student in this chapter, has taken the train from Newark, New Jersey to New York City several times. One year, he went with his family to Times Square to celebrate the New Year. Another time, they took the train to see the Lunar New Year celebrated in Chinatown. Stephen and his father also took the train so that they could go to the top of the Empire State Building.

In his mathematics class, Stephen is learning a formula for measuring the rate that a train travels from one point to another over a specified period of time. He finds it easy to connect this new math concept with his travel experiences from Newark to New York City.

Drawing from what we have discussed about learning as a sociocultural process, describe two reasons Stephen is finding it helpful to connect what he is learning with a personal experience.

_____

_____

_____

_____

_____

_____

In a great sense, Stephen's teacher, either serendipitously or intentionally, has connected learning with Stephen's sociocultural experiences to create a content-rich learning environment for him. An essential quest for all of us who teach is to build these types of personal, social, and cultural connections to learning with all of our students. The *what* we teach is an essential part of making sure that we are using culturally responsive practices by engaging students in experiences that tap into their experiences. Another feature of this element is that it also taps into issues that are socially relevant to who our students are. We will discuss this further in our next section.

2. **Learning is a linguistic process.** A second and no less important element is supporting students to communicate across all language domains (i.e., listening, speaking, reading, and writing) in the subject matters they are studying. Experts in language and learning Fang and Schleppegrell (2010), Freeman and Freeman (2009), and Halliday (1994, 2003) offer insights about the importance of providing students with explicit instruction on the following steps:
   a.   how subject-specific text (e.g., mathematics, science, and history books) is communicated in the four language domains;

b.   how to engage in subject-specific communication in classroom settings and elsewhere;

c.   how the language used to communicate relates to its meaning;

d.   how meaning is influenced by the context in which it is written or used; and

e.   how the context is influenced by a specific genre or medium.

Let's say, for example, that Stephen's teacher wants students in her class to write the formula for measuring a specific distance that a train will travel at a certain speed for a fixed period of time, such as how many miles a train will travel at 45 miles per hour for 2.5 hours. Matching the steps described above, she takes time to explain how this is written and writes on the board as she explains the ideas. She models how this type of mathematics about distance, rate, and time is spoken in her math class and elsewhere, and she then engages students in paired and group activities, where they listen and speak with their peers using this type of specialized or, in this example, subject-specific language. Stephen learns that the mathematical formula for the distance a person travels at a certain rate over a certain period of time is $d = \frac{r}{t}$. He learns that the formula represents a specific way that language is expressed in mathematics and that the academic vocabulary (*distance*, *rate*, and *time*) is used to express this subject-specific understanding. He then learns a similar type of math problem regarding measuring the amount of time it takes to travel at a certain rate over a period of time. Stephen's teacher repeats the same steps we stated earlier. She then assigns the following word problem that Stephen completes:

Example 2: Expression of a Math Problem about Time, Distance, and Rate

In a complete sentence, write the formula and solve the following problem:

> Shayla walks at a speed of 4 mph. How much time does she take to walk a distance of 20 miles?

Stephen's response is the following:

> *The mathematical formula for this problem is:* $t = \frac{d}{r}$ *, or* $t = \frac{20\ miles}{4\ mph}$*, and the answer is 5 hours.*

Fang and Shleppegrell (2010) also point to the importance of explicitly showing students the difference between how typical children's stories are written, using very simple text and non-technical vocabulary, versus how subject-specific text is written. For example, the popular children's story *Charlotte's Web* (White, 2006) begins with the type of simple text and non-technical vocabulary that is found in most children's stories. It begins as follows:

Example 3: Typical Children's Story

"Where's papa going with that ax?" said Fern to her mother as they were setting the table for breakfast" (White, 2006).

Compare Example 1 and Example 2 with the example we just referenced from the opening sentence of *Charlotte's Web*.

- Describe two to three key differences in the type of language that is used in the first two examples versus the third example.

  _____

  _____

  _____

- Describe two to three similarities in the type of language used in Example 1 and Example 2 that Stephen uses to express his mathematical understanding about distance, rate, and time.

  _____

  _____

  _____

- In what ways is the vocabulary in Examples 1 and 2 different from Example 3?

  _____

  _____

  _____

- Look at a sample sentence from an adult fiction book that you are reading for pleasure. How is it the same or different from the type of language that is used in our example from *Charlotte's Web*?

  _____

  _____

  _____

- Look at another sample sentence from an adult fiction book that you are reading for pleasure. How is it the same or different from the academic Examples 1 and 2?

  _____

  _____

  _____

Our reflection tasks were intended to support us in seeing the importance of providing explicit and direct instruction on how academic language is used in school settings and elsewhere, as it is so distinct from the simple text and non-technical vocabulary we are exposed to during pleasure reading and other activities that do not relate to *what* students learn in school settings.

Our instruction also requires that we understand the levels of literacy our students bring to the work of learning a specific subject so that we enact tasks and activities that build from their prior literacy experiences. For example, let's say that Stephen's teacher assumes incorrectly that he and the rest of his class are fluent in writing and solving math problems involving rate, distance, and time. With this false assumption, she writes the following on the smartboard: $t = \frac{d}{r}$, $r = \frac{d}{t}$, $d = \frac{r}{t}$. Adjacent to this, she writes five problems. One is: *Matt took a train from 8 a.m. to 3 p.m. at a rate of 45 miles an hour. If the train stopped for one hour, how many miles did the train travel?* She then tells students to solve the questions independently using the formulas. A few, including Stephen, attempt to do the task while the rest look blankly at the board and become very frustrated with what they perceive is their lack of math acumen. We meet with her after class to discuss the challenges she experienced. She laments that the task was too far over most students' heads and that she has to rethink the steps she will take to support their literacy in this type of math learning.

3. **Learning is an academic process.** Our third element involves supporting student learning of academic subject matter. While our second section on literacy as a developmental process looked at academic vocabulary, academic language learning requires that students be able understand the core concepts, or what some refer to as the overarching concepts, of the subject matter they are studying. The questions in Figure 3.5 exemplify some key overarching concepts that might be used to guide students' exploration of specific subject matter.

---

1. A kindergarten science class is exploring: "Why is the rainforest important to our planet?"
2. A high school English language arts class is exploring: "Why are main characters (1) who fight for something good and (2) who fight against something good an essential element in literature?"
3. A middle school mathematics class is exploring: "How is mathematics used to solve everyday problems?"
4. A high school U.S. history class is engaged in a unit of study on immigration. They are exploring: "What are the key reasons that people move from one place to another?"

Figure 3.5: Key Overarching Concepts

1. Write a detailed four- to five-sentence response to two of the four examples of overarching questions that we just asked.

    _____

    _____

    _____

    _____

    _____

    _____

2. Analyze your answer based on two criteria: (1) Were you able to express a robust amount of your knowledge of key academic content? (2) How was what you wrote reflective of the key goals and objectives represented on these subject matters?

    _____

    _____

    _____

    _____

    _____

    _____

There are three key tasks we must engage in to prepare students for academic learning. First, we must identify and define the objectives of a unit of study using student-friendly language so that everyone in our class understands them. Second, we must identify and assign tasks that students will do to express their understanding of the unit objectives (i.e., create a poster that describes five reasons why people move from one place to another). A third and no less important aspect of the academic-curricular element is supporting students to learn the key academic vocabulary, or the terms, words, idioms, and phrases [TWIPs] associated with the subject matter we are teaching (Zacarian, 2010).

4. **Learning is a cognitive process.** The fourth element involves how we can engage students in exploring how subject-matter language is used to express thinking. Many of us are familiar with Vygotsky's theories about cognition. We described them in our first chapter as being an interactive process that is socially constructed. Vygotsky theorized that learning to think and express our thinking is an active process that requires interactions. Renowned sociolinguist Michael Halliday (1994) looked closely at how we use language to express our thinking. Experts in language issues, bilingual education, and literacy Peregoy and Boyle (2017, 2008) drew from Halliday's understandings

of language expression to describe seven different ways that we use language to express something:

a. **Ask questions, ask for something:** For example, encouraging students to ask specific questions about what they are learning, such as "What is the definition of a rainforest?" and "Does the rainforest exist in the United States?

b. **Tell others what to do, control a situation, determine the sequence of events, and engage in a role-play that requires a level of authority or control:** For example, support each student to be a leader when engaging in group work by assigning the them the role of facilitator, whose assignment is to begin and end the group's discussion, summarize what the group has discussed, and plan next-step activities.

c. **Work in pairs or groups:** For example, paired and group work involves a high level of collaboration. When we look for evidence that each member is participating positively, it is helpful to proactively celebrate these communications.

d. **Express our feeling or personal experiences:** It is helpful to support students in sharing their feelings and experiences in an environment where they will feel safe and secure in their classroom community. It can be helpful for students to see that it is okay to make errors (Zacarian and Silverstone, 2020). An example is an elementary teacher who writes a solution to a mathematics problem on the board, realizes that he has made an error, and states the following aloud: "Aha, I think I made a mistake in my solution. I always think making mistakes is the way I learn best. I don't feel badly about it. I am happy when I see errors! Let's talk about the error that I think I made."

e. **Gain knowledge about the world in which we live through asking questions and explaining ideas:** An example of this is a student who asks how the sun supports the rainforest to thrive.

f. **Be creative using our own imaginations:** Students should have a voice and choice in their learning. An example of this is a history teacher who empowers small groups of students to describe the main reasons people move from one place to another by writing/acting out a play, writing a song, creating a poster, or conducting any creative presentation of their choosing.

g. **Convey facts and information:** For example, each of the examples that we provided in Figure 3.3 require students to engage in this language function by furnishing information about themselves.

Write seven different tasks that you might engage students, one for each function of language.

_____
_____
_____
_____
_____
_____
_____
_____
_____
_____

All of these language functions are critical in our classrooms. It's important to look carefully at *what* we are teaching to be sure that we engage students in the full complement of language functions to express their thinking.

It is also essential that students engage in challenging, thought-providing tasks to express their thinking. Zwiers (2012) provides us with a helpful way for doing this with sentence prompts and starters to engage students in academic conversations about what they are exploring. Examples of these include:

Prompts

- Can you give me an example of a ratio problem involving distance, rate, and time?
- How would you express that problem in a full sentence?

Responses

- In our math text, it says that . . .
- One example of this formula is . . .

Write a sentence prompt that our math teacher might use. _____
_____
_____
_____

Graphic or visual organizers are also helpful for supporting students to think to learn. For example, let's say that Stephan's science teacher asks her students to work with a partner and draw a visual listing of how the rainforest is different from the Sahara Desert. Some of her students might draw a Venn diagram like Figure 3.6:

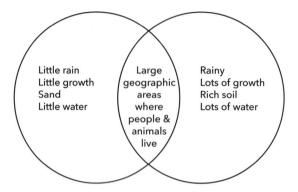

Figure 3.6: Venn Diagram to Illustrate Differences

Others might draw a list of the differences like the one depicted in the following list (Figure 3.7).

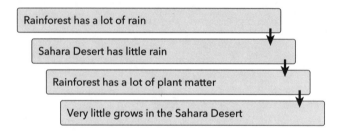

Figure 3.7: List to Depict Differences

What is key in using graphic organizers or visuals is that students are provided with ample ways to visually see what is being explored in a meaningful and comprehensible way. As such, it is very helpful to display how graphic organizers are used to express the thinking behind the concepts that we teach. Thinking maps are a set of eight different research-based visual tools used to describe the different ways we express our thinking (Hyerle, Curtis, & Alpert, 2004; Wikipedia, 2019). Here is a list and explanations of the eight different types of thinking that they ascribe.

1. **Brainstorming:** This is a type of open-ended question in which we ask students to share what they know, such as asking what students know about the rainforest. A visual shape that Hyerle, et al. (2004) uses to convey this is a

donut, where the hole or inside is labeled as the rainforest and the donut shape holds all of the information that's brainstormed about it.

2. **Describing:** Asking students to describe something engages them in a different kind of thinking act. Let's say that we ask to students to describe the rainforest. They might say something like: *It's full of plants; It's got a lot of water; A place where it rains a lot.* We might use a visual as a way for students to see the various descriptors. Some refer to the visual commonly used to describe this type of thinking as a bubble map (Wikipedia, 2019).

3. **Sequencing/ordering:** A type of visual for this is a timeline or flow chart of a process. For example, here are two flow charts (Figure 3.8 and Figure 3.9) depicting the same three decades:

Figure 3.8: Example 1 of a Flow Chart

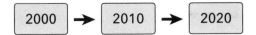

Figure 3.9: Example 2 of a Flow Chart

4. **Comparing/contrasting:** Many of us use visuals for displaying how things are different. Some use a Venn diagram and others use another type of visual for this type of thinking as we illustrated in Figures 3.6 and 3.7.

5. **Classifying/grouping:** Visualize a tree and its branches and roots. A tree diagram is a helpful way to represent the different structures of a concept. An example of a tree diagram is see in Figure 3.10.

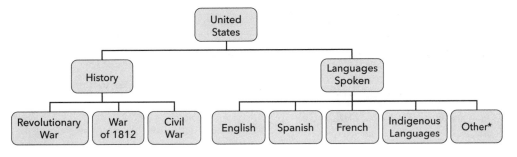

While many textbooks list the languages presented, additional languages were spoken including those of enslaved peoples and others.

Figure 3.10: Tree Chart Example

A visual representation of a hierarchy that shows the process or steps that lead to the big picture, such as in Figure 3.11, can be a very helpful means for students to see to understand.

Figure 3.11: Example of a Whole-to-Part Relationship:

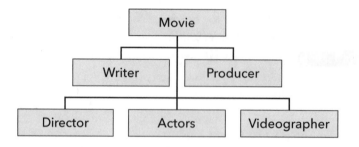

Describing cause-effect relationships: Many teachers use a visual, such as Figure 3.12 below, to show the cause and effect of an event.

Figure 3.12: Example of a Visual Chart:

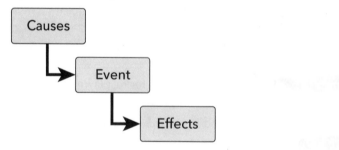

Seeing analogies: According to Hyerle, a visual can be used to show the relationships between one topic or idea and another, along with the factors that relate the two. An example would be to use a visual, such as Figure 3.13, for the following analogy: *Boiling is to freezing as elderly is to infancy*:

Figure 3.13: Visual Example:

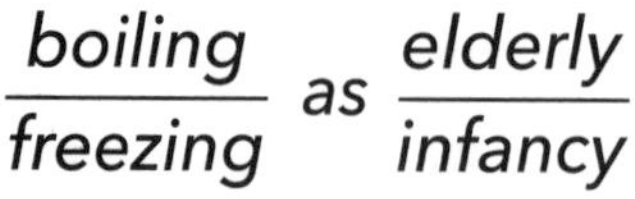

$$\frac{boiling}{freezing} \; as \; \frac{elderly}{infancy}$$

BUILDING DEEPER CONNECTIONS BY CONNECTING TO ISSUES OF SOCIAL JUSTICE AND EQUITY

Thus far in this chapter, we have described various culturally responsive approaches to education by looking at the *who* and *what* we teach. In addition, it is crucial to consider how we can connect the curriculum and approaches we use to teach to issues of social justice and equity so that we are more secure in using anti-bias, anti-racist practices. These approaches help us to support students to make our school communities and even society more just and take care of our planet by continuously engaging students in practicing the ideals of democracy. An ideal place for students to learn about, see models of, and apprentice into culturally responsive practices is their classroom and school.

One of the most powerful ways for infusing these practices is in applying what we hope students will learn into what they do to learn. Take, for example, the mathematics teacher who is teaching a unit on distance, rate, and time. Thus far, we have seen that she has connected Stephen's experience riding the train from Newark to New York City to the unit of study. Let's take a social justice issue, such as offering high-speed trains in certain areas over others and how this benefits some groups and not others (e.g., people who live in big cities versus people who live in smaller cities). Almost every subject matter has a way to link it to a social justice issue students can examine. Another example is the unit of study that Stephen and his classmates are working on in their geology class. Their teacher has been connecting the unit of study with fracking, a technique used to harvest gas, and supporting her students to explore issues of interest to everyone, including air, soil, and water pollution as well as the possibility that fracking may cause earthquakes. Supporting students to examine curricular issues that are relevant to their lives is a key means to spark their interest to learn, see real and applicable meaning in learning, and sustain their interest in continuing to learn.

Look back at Figure 3.5: Key Overarching Concepts. Connect each overarching concept (there are four) and the associated grade level it is intended for to a social justice issue students might explore.

_____

_____

_____

_____

_____

_____

Our next chapter will explore the importance of family–school engagement.

4

Building Culturally Responsive
Family–School Partnerships

WHEN THE JIMENEZ FAMILY immigrated to the United States from Ecuador, they immediately enrolled their children in their local school, but found themselves alienated from a schooling system they didn't understand. In her home country, Mrs. Jimenez visited her children's school and classroom often, but in the United States, she found the school inaccessible. This was due to both the language divide as well as the lack of warmth she felt every morning when she dropped her children off at school. One day when Mrs. Jimenez was speaking to Ms. Sanchez, one of the few Spanish-speaking teachers on campus, she learned that the district had recently started offering a parent and family engagement program called Project 2Inspire. Upon learning this, Mrs. Jimenez beamed with joy, as she was hopeful that this was a way for her to feel more connected to the school community and ensure that her children were getting the schooling they deserved.

In this chapter, we describe a promising practice, Project 2Inspire, to highlight some of the essential principles and practices for building culturally responsive family–school partnerships. These include:

- Community Learning Theory,
- the Unity Principle,
- Co-powerment, and
- Model for Parental Involvement.

Before we launch into a description of the principled thinking of the Project 2Inspire model created by the California Association of Bilingual Education (CABE), it's helpful to take stock of the type of parent engagement and empowerment models we currently have so that we can see the inspiration that grounded Project 2Inspire. First, partnerships should not be seen as an extra add-on to what we do. Regardless of where we work and what we do, we should be partnering with the very people who have the most interest, the most love for, and the most investment in our students— their parents. Whether our students are being raised by two parents, a single parent, grandparents, foster parents, siblings, unrelated people living cooperatively, or with extra familial supports, family engagement is at the core of our work. Indeed, we use the words *parents* and *families* interchangeably to refer to those who are the primary caregivers for our students and who greatly support their development. It's helpful to also describe the distinctions that we see between family involvement and family engagement versus what we will later describe as family co-powerment. As Ferlazzo (2011) suggests, "One of the dictionary definitions of *involve* is 'to enfold or envelope,' whereas one of the meanings of *engage* is 'to come together and interlock.'" Thus, *involvement* implies *doing to*; in contrast, *engagement* implies *doing with*.

Let's look at some of the key foundational differences between what we describe as family involvement and engagement. Involvement, to us, can be a misleading word when it comes to the essential work of partnering closely with families. Why do we say this? The act of being involved does not necessarily mean that one is active, participatory, or an equal member in doing something or in taking an action. Take, for example, a parent who attends a parent-teacher conference by taking precious time away from work and/or precious monies to pay a childcare provider to come to us. At the conference, they might sit passively while we take up all of the meeting time to report what their child is doing in school. While the parent is somewhat involved at the meeting by being the listener, that type of involvement is not really an equal or participatory action of being. Engagement is a very different form of activity. It requires that parents be active and participatory and that they engage in the same degree of input as educators do because it is a participatory action. And, engagement expects and even anticipates this high level of co-equal participation on behalf of our students. While we discuss the principles of co-powerment later in this chapter, we want to lay the foundation of it by grounding families as equal, participatory partners.

According to family engagement experts Henderson, Mapp, Johnson, and Davies (2007), there is an abundance of research which points to the critical importance of the type of family–school engagement to which we are referring. However, we also want to share that while the evidence is clear, when it comes to communities of color,

Families should be equal, participatory partners.

Involved vs. Engagement
passive   active participant
non participant

harder to engage those who have been disenfranchised

particularly people who may come from countries other than the United States or who have traditionally or more recently been further disenfranchised from participating in our institutions, becoming involved may be much more challenging than we might think it is. In addition, we may inadvertently distance ourselves from the very people who most value and would most welcome the type of partnerships we describe in this chapter.

In this chapter, we show evidence that when we work together to overcome barriers to parent participation, students' engagement in school and social-emotional and academic success are much more realized. Underlying our vision for this as a culturally responsive practice is a strong belief that schools can be much more successful for all students when we create true and lasting relationships grounded in a core belief in partnerships. Let's begin by looking at the foundational underpinnings of Project 2Inspire.

THE ROOTS OF PROJECT 2INSPIRE

For the past 13 years, the California Association for Bilingual Education's (CABE) Parent and Family Engagement Program has been focused on implementing strong family and community engagement sessions that build leadership capacity and value and draw upon community funds of knowledge to inform, support, and enhance teaching and learning for all students so that they can graduate college and obtain a career using 21st-century skills. These programs were developed in order to search for the best way to serve parent communities, as well as to design a culturally responsive program for communities of color. CABE's multifaceted Parent and Family Engagement Program focuses on working with its partners from school districts and county offices to provide parents with the best opportunities and resources to help their children succeed in school. To achieve this goal, its Parent and Family Engagement Program:

- provides high-quality education, resources, and leadership development to ALL parents; and
- offers professional development for district and school administrators, parent involvement coordinators or liaisons, and other family engagement professionals on research-based strategies and effective practices, which include the Community Learning Theory and the Model for Parental Involvement, described later in this chapter.

1. What kinds of parental engagement programs have you experienced or seen provided?

_____

_____

_____

2. What do you see as the primary purpose of these?

_____

_____

_____

3. How do the parent engagement programs you described in responses 1 and 2 pay particular attention to communities of color and/or families living in poverty or living with adversity?

_____

_____

_____

4. What are some ways you might try to engage a parent like Mrs. Jimenez in your classroom?

_____

_____

_____

One of the many programs CABE offers on parent and family engagement is Project 2Inspire. It is a comprehensive, research-based collaborative project that uses a school-based systemic approach to build the capacity of schools and districts in establishing a Family–School–Community Leadership Program that involves families, community-based organizations, teachers, administrators, other school staff, and stakeholders. The goal of the program is to provide parents, teachers, community liaisons, and principals with the tools they need to work together as partners to improve schools and support the education of their children.

Project 2Inspire includes three sequential levels of programming: awareness, mastery, and expert. When Mrs. Jimenez joined the Project 2Inspire program, she began at the awareness level. It included 12 modules, each lasting 1.5 hours, with a focus on information impacting her children. In the succeeding two years, Mrs. Jimenez advanced to the mastery and expert levels. The three levels—awareness, mastery, and expert—are designed so that districts and/or schools that invest in the program will build "parent experts" who have the capacity to continue the work. Once parent expertise has been acquired, schools and/or districts may choose to hire such parents to continue the program and obtain sustainability.

Here is a description of the three levels of parent leadership offerings schools and districts may choose to provide. It is important to note that these are offered at times during the day that are determined to work the most successfully for the majority of a community's parents.

1. **Awareness Level**
   - 12 modules – 1.5 hours each
   - information impacting their children
   - offered at district level or at school sites and at CABE conference; parents can attend a varying number of sessions

2. **Mastery Level**
   - 12 modules – 3 hours each
   - in-depth understanding of critical information impacting their children
   - participant-centered and significantly more intensive in terms of content (deeper coverage), time, and effort
   - participants are required to complete all 12 training modules, for a total of 36 hours of face-to-face, project-based learning activities

3. **Expert Level**
   - 16 modules – 3 hours each
   - participants must have completed mastery level
   - development and refinement of leadership knowledge and skills to create and sustain family–school community engagement in supporting student achievement
   - parent leadership development effort that builds upon the knowledge and skills developed in level 2 (mastery) training
   - parents/community liaisons completing the program may offer services to other parents in their schools

LAUNCHING PROJECT 2INSPIRE AND RESEARCHING ITS EFFICACY

To understand Project 2Inspire, let's look at its grounding principles. In 2003, Maria Quezada, former CABE CEO and creator of the Project 2Inspire program, submitted a proposal for a Parent Information Resource Center (PIRC) grant from the U.S. Department of Education's Office of Innovation and Improvement and obtained grant funding for the development of the Project 2Inspire program. In 2006, CABE secured a second PIRC grant with a statewide focus in order to further develop the parent engagement program. The second federal grant included funding to conduct research on family engagement, which gave CABE the opportunity to design a culturally responsive program for communities of color (explained further below) and to determine the impact the program was having on parents and their children's academic achievement.

The Research Study

Eighteen treatment schools and 18 control schools were randomly selected to participate in this study. The control schools did not receive any of the sessions that were provided in the treatment schools. Parents at the 18 treatment schools received 12 three-hour modules at the mastery level and 18 three-hour modules at the trainer-of-trainers expert level. The question that guided the research was the following: Did the students whose parents attended the mastery- and expert-level sessions have an increase in achievement?

Findings from the Research

The study showed that the treatment schools did have significant achievement growth and parental engagement over other students at the control schools. An additional finding, and one that it quite relevant to include as it relates to students' academic learning, is that English learners whose parents attended the parent leadership development sessions also learned more English than did students at the treatment schools whose parents hadn't attended the program sessions, as measured by the gains on the California English Language Development Test (Quezada, 2016). According to Quezada (2016):

> When we used this culturally responsive process, we were inspired by the transformation experienced by the parents attending our institutes—especially after they had attended several sessions. Parents who never shared or participated in the early discussions would freely and confidently do so during the final sessions; parents shared that they were more active in ensuring their child was getting on track for college. We were creating and fostering a sense of community, belonging, and personal power among the parents attending the sessions. Project staff developed a greater understanding of the families and became more adept at addressing the cultural, linguistic, social, economic, and political barriers they faced. They created activities that engaged parents through the use of art and metaphors, creating a safe place to share their lives and aspirations for their children. The parents recognized that we were reaching out to them in a very different way than schools usually did.

Mrs. Jimenez benefitted from Project 2Inspire in many of the ways suggested by Quezada: she found her voice and was explicitly taught about the American schooling system, as well as how to advocate for herself and her children. As a result of Project 2Inspire, Mrs. Jimenez was also hired as a parent liaison, where she will offer Project 2Inspire trainings to other parents at her school and in her district. If we look back at Mrs. Jimenez, we see that she initially believed the school was inaccessible to her and that she was not welcome there.

Describe three to four actions you believe supported Mrs. Jimenez to be empowered as an active contributory parent in her children's school.

_____
_____
_____
_____
_____
_____

PROJECT 2INSPIRE TRAINER OF TRAINERS (TOT)

In addition to the Parent Leadership offerings for parents, Project 2Inspire also includes a Trainer of Trainers (TOT) module for staff and district personnel to strengthen a school and district's capacity to partner with families. This four-day Trainer of Trainers module for school staff and district personnel focuses on:

- increasing the capacity of districts/schools to provide outreach to and engage parents meaningfully in a program that has attained a high level of success in schools throughout California; and
- school staff and district personnel completing the program so that they may offer services to other parents in their schools and districts.

The Trainer of Trainers modules have extended CABE's thinking about the power of partnerships among the various participants. After completing and reflecting on the first two PIRC grants, for example, CABE decided to add trainings for all of the stakeholders, including school staff and district personnel. This became increasingly important as administrators began seeing many positive changes in parents, such as Mrs. Jimenez, at their school sites but didn't understand how the changes came about fully. As Quezada suggests, "They spoke of how the parents were 'changing the dynamics' of teacher-to-parent interactions and that parents had learned how to communicate effectively with them, so they were able to express their views about what changes were needed at the school." As such, in 2012, CABE applied for and obtained an Investing in Innovation (i3) development grant and incorporated school staff and district personnel into the program, with an emphasis on fostering relationships among the principal, teachers, and other parents, as well as the development of a yearly plan for parental engagement where parents help plan, monitor, and evaluate the plan.

A typical TOT sequence now includes the following schedule and content:

- a two-day session on parent engagement research, strategies, and practices;
- a two-day session on cultural proficiency in schools based on research by noted experts (Michelle Brooks, Karen Mapp, and Randall Lindsay); and
- a two-day session for school staff and district personnel on the Action Team for Partnerships (ATP) model, where participants collectively write their action plan for parent engagement by drawing from Epstein et al (2001) for their school.

1. **Describe two or three key differences between Project 2Inspire and other parental engagement programs you are familiar with.**

   _____

   _____

   _____

2. **Looking at the ways in which Project 2Inspire studied its own efficacy, what evidence-based strategies might you use to implement a parent engagement program?**

   _____

   _____

   _____

   _____

KEY PRINCIPLES GROUNDING PROJECT 2INSPIRE
AND BUILDING CULTURALLY RESPONSIVE SCHOOLS

Project 2Inspire was created based on some key theoretical principles for parents and family engagement. These include Community Learning Theory, the Unity Principle, co-powerment, and the Model for Parental Involvement. Let's look closely at each of these principles so that we may understand how they also ground what we believe is essential for building culturally responsive family–school partnerships.

Community Learning Theory

The Project 2Inspire program is grounded in Community Learning Theory (CLT), developed by Roberto Vargas (2008) and J. David Ramirez (2010). It is a cultural strategy that uses diversity-responsive processes and activities that are foundational for developing the critical relationships needed for individual and community empowerment, action, and change. At its very core, CLT is a deep and unrelenting belief in the power of the strengths and assets everyone brings to the possibilities of learning and growing together on behalf of our shared purpose in supporting the success of our students in school and in their lives. CLT's guiding principles include:

- building a process/approach that builds among participants communities of mutual support and trust for collaboration;
- creating group environments that promote dialogue and reflection and encourage positive action;
- creating environments that nurture parents' ability to transform their empathy and learning into action (i.e., developing trusting relationships, co-powering, and advancing positive changes for the home, school, and community);
- valuing every person for who they are as well as what they bring through their many experiences in order to build meaningful relationships based on trust and respect (e.g., parent and parent, parent and teacher, parent and administrator);
- fostering, in every person and group, a sense of self, place, purpose, direction, possibilities, and options, and believing that every person and group has the capacity for self-discovery, improvement, shared learning, and action; and
- validating the fact that every group of people has the potential of becoming a learning circle that shares wisdom, creates group knowledge, and fosters personal growth.

The CLT approach also includes acknowledging and building on existing cultural funds of knowledge, or what Yosso (2005) and others call "community cultural wealth." According to Yosso (2005), cultural wealth includes both *ventajas* (assets or personal resources) and what Anzaldúa (1999) calls *conocimiento* (knowledge or awareness that evolves through specific life experiences). Yosso's framework includes six forms of cultural wealth:

1. aspirational,
2. linguistic,
3. familial,
4. social,
5. navigational, and
6. resistant.

Additionally, researchers Kanagala, Rendón, and Nora (2016) have also uncovered four additional forms of *ventajas y conocimiento:*

1. g*anas*/perseverance,
2. ethnic consciousness,
3. spirituality/faith, and
4. pluriversal cultural wealth.

Each of the 10 forms of cultural wealth were described by students in a research project by Kanagala, Rendón, and Nora (2016). Let's look at their descriptions:

1. **Aspirational Wealth:** Students shared that they were optimistic about their futures and that their aspirations were shaped by their families, who validated them, and shared *tesimonios*/life stories and *consejos*/sage advice.
2. **Linguistic Wealth:** Students recognized that being bilingual was an asset and that their bilingualism allowed them to communicate both personally and professionally.
3. **Familial Wealth:** The family unit, especially mothers, provided crucial support. Students wanted to complete life goals for themselves and their families.
4. **Social Wealth:** Students relied on a strong social network, which included mostly Latino/a friends and peers.
5. **Navigational Wealth:** Students learned how to navigate multiple contexts, which required its own norms and expectations.
6. **Resistant Wealth:** Students acquired resilience in the midst of microaggressions and culture shock, and they learned to challenge inequities.
7. *Ganas*/**Perseverant Wealth:** Students refused to quit and they were able to overcome difficult challenges.
8. **Ethnic Consciousness Wealth:** Shared experiences of inequity allowed students to give back to their communities and to be proud of their heritage.
9. **Spiritual/Faith-based Wealth:** Students had a strong belief system in God, had a sense of purpose, and a positive view of the world.
10. **Pluriversal Wealth:** Students were able to successfully move in and out of multiple social and intellectual spaces, which allowed them to remain flexible and open to change.

Throughout the Project 2Inspire program, Mrs. Jimenez was able to share her own *ventajas* (assets or personal resources) and *conocimiento* (knowledge or awareness that evolves through specific life experiences), which made her feel part of the community and professional learning process. Specifically, Mrs. Jimenez shared *testimonios*/life stories about overcoming adversity by leaving her home country and starting a new life in the United States, as well as the sacrifices she made for her children's benefit. She also shared *consejos*/sage advice with new Project 2Inspire parents regarding how to acclimate to the United States and a new schooling system. Lastly, Mrs. Jimenez shared how she modeled for her children *ganas*/perserverance by not giving up during difficult financial times. Instead, she explained the sacrifices she made by working two jobs and the discipline she demonstrated by being willing to go the extra mile at work and eventually being promoted.

1. What kinds of *ventajas* (assets or personal resources) and *conocimiento* (knowledge or awareness that evolves through specific life experiences) might the parents in your community share with the school community?

    _____

    _____

    _____

    _____

2. What kinds of *ventajas* (assets or personal resources) and *conocimiento* (knowledge or awareness that evolves through specific life experiences) can you share with your own students?

    _____

    _____

    _____

    _____

The Unity Principle

The Project 2Inspire program also introduces Vargas's (1987) concepts of the Unity Principle, which seeks to build a sense of *conocimiento* ("Who am I?," "Who are they?," and "Who are we?") and unity through shared power and trust. Vargas further describes the Conocimiento Principle as " . . . recognizing that common unity begins with the process of shared awareness and understanding, or *conocimiento*. In essence, we must learn the basics of who each person is before we can evolve the trust and bonding required for unity and shared group power. With this principle in mind, all group efforts balance the focus on a task with a conscious effort to maximize relationships of shared awareness among participants." As such, meetings are started by communicating the equal values of becoming a community and the task to be accomplished. There are shared introductions, the modeling of "Who am I?" by the facilitator, and the use of smaller groups or even dyads (or pairs) for doing *conocimiento* or working on the task. For example, a meeting might start with everyone going around the room and sharing who they are as a parent or parent leader. Using this process, Mrs. Jimenez and other parents involved in Project 2Inspire learned more about each person they were working with, as well as the lived experiences that have given them cultural capital and wisdom now shared with others. Knowing individuals at a deeper level brings *confianza* (confidence and trust) to work together in unity and power. The Unity Principle begins by viewing and understanding parents from an asset model and as equal partners who can co-construct and co-contribute knowledge within a system.

1. Why might it be important to begin with the unity principle and *conocimiento* with parents?

_____

_____

_____

_____

2. How might you be able to use the unity principle and *conocimiento*?

_____

_____

_____

Co-Powerment

In his work in communities, Vargas (2008) has also introduced the concept of co-powerment, a practice that he believes is:

> "more collaborative than the hierarchical relationships often implied by the idea of empowerment. . . . Co-powerment is communication that seeks to lift the confidence, energy, and agency of another person, self, and the relationship. It is lifting the power of self and others. The better we become at co-powering, the more we grow deeper relationships that develop our power to create positive personal, family, and community change."

Mrs. Jimenez was inspired by the concept of co-powerment, and, as a district-level parent liaison, it began to transform her family and her workplace. She began to use some of the same skills that she learned via Project 2Inspire when she was promoted as a manager. She found that she wanted a less hierarchical relationship with those that she supervised, and so she began using many of the same exercises she learned throughout the program with her staff, such as having employees share their *conocimiento* and *testimonios*. In this way, the unity principle and co-powerment are intended to change one's entire community and not merely oneself.

1. What kind of shift do you notice between empowerment and co-powerment?

    _____
    _____
    _____

2. How might you be able to build co-powerment with students and parents?

    _____
    _____
    _____

Before the Project 2Inspire program, Mrs. Jimenez encountered many issues and misunderstandings with teachers and administrators regarding her role in school. In addition, although she wanted to be an involved parent as she had been in Ecuador, she often felt judged for not doing enough *and* was never explicitly told what the school community expected of her. Her experiences are critical to consider as we create culturally responsive practices with families. Family engagement experts Henderson et al (2007), Mapp (2014), Henderson and Dahm (2013), and Henderson (n.d.) provide a helpful way for assessing our own experiences and the schools in which we work. In their renowned book aptly titled *Beyond the Bake Sale: The Essential Guide to Family-School Partnerships,* Henderson et al. (2007) describe four types of schools. Each type describes the varying degrees of partnership accessibility that parents experience working with schools. The four range in intensity from schools who keep parents out to schools who embrace the totality of a co-powered approach.

1. Describe the type of family–school partnership that is the most familiar to you (either that you attended or that you have worked or currently work at).

    _____
    _____
    _____
    _____

2. Drawing from the theoretical principles that we presented thus far, including Community Learning Theory, the Unity Principle, and co-powerment, what might the school you described do to create a stronger and more successful culture of responsiveness, whereby parents such as Mrs. Jimenez are true partners on behalf of their children's academic and social-emotional learning and engagement in school?

    _____
    _____
    _____
    _____

Since the date of Henderson and colleagues' seminal publication, their work has continued to contribute greatly to our current thinking about the types of schools in which we work. They are often invited to speak and write to amplify the importance of our engaging in the types of examinations we just employed in our reflection tasks (Mapp, 2014, Henderson, n.d., and Henderson and Dahm, 2013).

Model for Parental Involvement

The Project 2Inspire program is also influenced by the work of Joyce Epstein of Johns Hopkins University. Renowned for her research and contributions in family–school engagement, she developed the Model for School, Family, and Community Partnerships (1995, 2009, 2019). It has two main components: spheres of influence and six types of involvement. The key concept that underlies both parts of this model is that all stakeholders in a child's education have mutual interests and influences. The primary shared interest is a caring concern that the child be successful. Additionally, the model suggests that stakeholders' shared interests and influences can be promoted by the policies, actions, beliefs, attitudes, and values of the stakeholders.

Epstein's Overlapping Spheres of Influence

Epstein's model differs from earlier theories on school–family relationships and revises earlier conceptualizations that viewed families and schools as existing in separate spheres, which required that they have separate responsibilities. It also revises conceptions of the school-family relationship as one that must be sequential. Sequential school-family relationships refer to sequential responsibilities of educating a child—home acting as the first educational environment and parents preparing their children to enter school, and later schools fully taking over the educational responsibilities (Epstein, 2001, p. 26). Thus, the sequential approach looks at the two entities, school and home, as separate and apart rather than as one important unit to support a child's growth and development.

Both of these assertions—separate responsibilities that are sequential—were areas of frustration for Mrs. Jimenez with the school community, as they are more individualistic and less communally oriented, which is what she was used to in her home country. In a sequential relationship, parents are expected to have more of a role than schools, and vice versa, in certain periods of a child's life. Mrs. Jimenez yearned for a partnership she could create with the school community so that she didn't feel so alone as she and her son were acclimating to the United States and their school community. Epstein's Model for Parental Involvement acknowledges that schools and families often do have more or less influence at certain ages and suggests that the overlap between families and schools can be increased with concerted effort by one or more of the stakeholders (Epstein, 2018).

1. How do or how would the spheres of influence impact your work with students and parents?

    _____

    _____

    _____

2. How does or how would the erroneous notion that schools and families have separate responsibilities that are sequential impact your work and understanding of parental involvement?

    _____

    _____

    _____

At its most extreme, the type of imbalance that can occur between families whose collectivist cultural frame of reference welcomes and embraces parent involvement versus what Henderson et al (2007), Henderson & Dahm (2013), Mapp (2014), and educators who value the merits of a *fortress school* is thoroughly weighted against any type of meaningful engagement. Let's say, for example, that we work in a fortress school. What would our beliefs about family engagement look like? Here are some examples of a fortress school.

- Families should be separate from and not partners with educators.
- The curriculum that is to be learned is the sole purview of teachers and not families.
- Issues of difference are not relevant; rather, the American English–speaking curriculum is of utmost importance, and it is more important to treat every family and student exactly the same.
- School personnel should only involve the parents that decide to support it.

At the extreme end of the spectrum, perhaps it is clear why this type of involvement will not and does not work because its drawbacks are so easy to identify. Let's look at an example of the extreme we are highlighting. Let's say that you are the parents of a profoundly deaf child and are deaf as well. You go to school and find that it makes no accommodations for your child or for you to participate. In its words and deeds, it tells you that "it can't deal with deafness." In a real sense, you would know that that school is not open to any of the many assets and strengths that you possess. However, schools, like any institution, are not an extreme good or bad; rather, we can keep falling into that in-between zone. Achieving that just-right balance of being culturally responsible means that we have to be willing to embrace the possibilities of partnerships by doing more than continue to evolve through all of our words and deeds with families. According to Mapp (2014), a true *partnership school* is one in which

> "All family activities are connected to learning; there is a clear and open process for resolving problems; parent networks are valued and cultivated; families are actively involved in decisions on school improvement; staff conduct intentional relationship-building events such as home visits to families."

Six Types of Parental Involvement

Epstein has also developed a framework for defining six different types of parental involvement, which the Project 2Inspire program has incorporated into their professional learning series. This framework assists educators in developing school and family partnership programs. She suggests, "When parents, teachers, students, and others view one another as partners in education, a caring community forms around students and begins its work" (Epstein, 2001). In a more recent description of the model, Epstein (2019) describes the model as a means to " . . . think purposefully about selecting activities that enable all families to become engaged in their child's education at home, at school, or in the community" (2019). Her description is based on years of research on this crucial topic. Epstein, one of the foremost experts in family engagement, conducted a study in 1981 about parents' perceptions of their child's school and teachers (1986). The findings from that study are as relevant today as they were many decades ago. Not surprisingly, they are often cited in the research on family engagement. Following is a summary of that study. As you read it, think of the implications that it has on your working environment.

Epstein created a questionnaire that was administered to "parents of 1,269 students in 82 first, third, and fifth grade classrooms in Maryland" (1986, p. 278). Of the 59% return in the total number of surveys, the results showed that parents felt positively about their child's school and teachers. In addition, however, it showed that parents felt that schools could do more to involve parents to support their child's learning, that a large number of parents felt "excluded" from "even the most basic traditional communications from the schools," and that "few parents were involved in the schools" (p. 290). Studies such as that seminal one, as well as the ones we have cited about its benefits on parent engagement and students' academic success, call for a transformation in our thinking about the importance of family involvement. It also should urgently help us to be laser focused on the six types of involvement Epstein describes.

Returning to Mrs. Jimenez, she worked her way through all three levels of the

Project 2Inspire program. During these, she was introduced to and practiced all six types of parental involvement. She was then able to teach and model these with the parents with whom she worked. The following section defines the six types of involvement framework, lists sample practices or activities, and provides a detailed example to describe the involvement more fully.

1. **Parenting: Help all families establish home environments to support children as students.**

   Sample Practices
   - suggestions for home conditions that support learning at each grade level;
   - workshops, videotapes, and computerized phone messages on parenting and child rearing at each age and grade level;
   - parent education and other courses or training for parents (e.g., GED, college credit, family literacy);
   - family support programs to assist families with health, nutrition, and other services;
   - home visits at transition points to preschool, elementary school, middle school, and high school; and
   - neighborhood meetings to help families understand schools and to help schools understand families.

     Example of a Home Visit: Second-grade teacher, Mr. Gold, and a group of educators from his elementary school wanted to support a group of what they described as at-risk students to continue to engage in pleasure reading during the summer break from school. Using monies from a small grant for this purpose, they worked with students and their families to assemble a list of books that the students expressed interest in reading. Each week through the summer months, Mr. Silverstone visited each home of the children with whom he worked. During the first meeting, he brought ice cream to share with the family along with a book. Over the ice cream treat, Mr. Silverstone noted how truly special it was to be a guest in their home and he shared this feeling with families. He demonstrated how he reads at home and explained that he begins by finding a place where he is comfortable. While almost all of his visits were in large bustling apartment complexes, each family welcomed his visit and expressed their excitement for his return. He began his first visit after the family enjoyed the treat by showing his student and an interested parent how he begins to read a new book by looking at the front cover and the title of the book to think about what the book might be about. He tells them that sometimes he asks himself questions like, "I wonder if the book is about . . ." They then begin to read the first few pages of the book. Each visit ends with some questions about what to do next and a plan for either finishing the book and talking about it during the next visit and beginning another book or continuing to read the one he brought.

2. **Communicating: Design effective forms of school-to-home and home-to-school communications about school programs and children's progress.**

   Sample Practices

   - conferences with every parent at least once a year, with follow-ups as needed;
   - language translators to assist families as needed;
   - weekly or monthly folders of student work sent home for review and comments;
   - parent/student pickup of report card, with conferences on improving grades;
   - regular schedule of useful notices, memos, phone calls, newsletters, and other communications; clear information on choosing schools or courses, programs, and activities within schools; and
   - clear information on all school policies, programs, reforms, and transitions. *Example:* Middle school social studies teacher Mr. Ahearn knows that family dialogue journals (FDJs) are one of the more recent innovations for supporting student, family, and teacher communications (Allen, Beaty, Dean, Jones, Smith Mathew, McCreight, Schwedler, & Simmons, 2015). Renowned expert in educational psychology/early childhood development Luis Moll describes FDJs as a way to "share our lives, experiences, and opinions" with others (2015, p. vii). One of the key ways to do this is what Mr. Ahearn does. He and his students are studying patterns of immigration in the U.S. Collaboratively, they form a sentence prompt to ask a family member or friend based on what they are studying. They are doing this to extend the conversation about what they are learning at home. Here is the prompt they created: *This week, we are learning about immigration and studying why people move from one place to another. Why do you think some people move from their homeland?*

   FDJs such as the one that Mr. Ahearn's class is engaging in help to create an authentic connection between home and school, help families to learn about what their child is studying, and are an innovative way for families to share their thoughts with their child in writing. However, of the 30 students in Mr. Ahearn's class, he knows that he might have some who are English learners and others who might be sight impaired. In these situations and others, he simply asks students to record their responses. He also encourages students to write in their home languages with their families or friends. He has found FDJs to be an essential component to his work.

3. **Volunteering: Recruit and organize parent help and support.**

   Sample Practices

   - school and classroom volunteer program to help teachers, administrators, students, and other parents;
   - parent room or family center for volunteer work, meetings, resources for families;
   - annual postcard survey to identify all available talents, times, and locations of volunteers;
   - class parent, telephone tree, or other structures to provide all families with needed information; and
   - parent patrols or other activities to aid in safety and operation of school programs.

   Example: At the very beginning of the school year, high school chemistry teacher Mrs. Peters sends a message to parents soliciting their involvement in her class. She tells them about the first unit of study that their children will be studying. Using as little chemistry terminology as possible, so that parents will be comfortable coming to her class, she asks parents to come to her class to demonstrate what they do for work or a hobby. During the unit on thermal reactions, for example, a parent who works in an optical shop came to class to demonstrate how he fixed broken wire-rimmed glasses. He brought a small torch and some gold and silver soldering wire and welded the broken pieces back together. It was a wonderful opportunity for the parent to authentically make students' studies come alive, helped students see how the ideas are used in a variety of occupations (including his), and had the ancillary but no less important benefit of helping his child to feel special, to see value in what his father does for work, and to see how special it was for his father to take time from work on behalf of his son.

4. **Learning at home: Provide information and ideas to families about how to help students at home with homework and other curriculum-related activities, decisions, and planning.**

   Sample Practices

   - information for families on skills required for students in all subjects at each grade;
   - information on homework policies and how to monitor and discuss schoolwork at home;
   - information on how to assist students to improve skills on various class and school assessments;

- regular schedule of homework that requires students to discuss and interact with families on what they are learning in class;
- calendars with activities for parents and students at home;
- family math, science, and reading activities at school;
- summer learning packets or activities; and
- family participation in setting student goals each year and in planning for college or work.

   Example: Third-grade teacher, Mr. Russell is supporting his students in fluidly performing addition tasks with ease. He holds periodic math game nights to teach families simple games that can be played at home to engage his students in these mental math tasks outside of class. Most recently, the parents of his students came to learn how to play the game cribbage. During the game night, he shares the rules of the game, models the games with a partner, and engages families to play the game. He explains how the game is connected to using number sense and looking for whole-to-part patterns.

5. **Decision-making: Include families as participants in school decisions and develop parent leaders and representatives.**

   Sample Practices
   - active Parent Teacher Association/Organization (PTA/PTO) or other parent groups, advisory councils, or committees (e.g., curriculum, safety, personnel) for parent leadership and participation;
   - independent advocacy groups to lobby and work for school reform and improvements;
   - district-level councils and committees for family and community involvement;
   - information on school or local elections for school representatives; and
   - networks to link all families with parent representatives.

   Example: Mrs. Rodrigues is a bilingual teacher in a K–6 elementary school that had been feverishly attempting to engage more parents in participating in its parent council as part of its school improvement efforts. In the past, it had attempted to do so by seeking families in its school newsletter and speaking with parents who were known to staff. It led to the same parents being involved in the councils year after year. Mrs. Rodrigues, a bilingual bicultural member of the community, suggested a creative way to recruit parents to the councils. She suggested that students perform a play in Spanish, the home language of about 30 students in a school of 250. While the staff thought this was a good idea, they worried that few would be interested as so few spoke Spanish. Mrs. Rodrigues suggested that such an event would help them to get to know some families and encourage them to participate in the school. She gathered the support of her fellow Spanish-speaking colleagues, the school principal, and some American English-speaking colleagues. They arranged for after-school tryouts for students in grades three through six, knowing that they would accept anyone who expressed an interest. By the end of the week, it seemed as if every third-through sixth-grade student tried out! Additional roles and a chorus had to be created to accommodate the numbers. Parents that had never participated in the school's activities volunteered to sew the costumes, make food, and, more importantly, bring the families to the performance. The play was held at various times after school and in the early evening. As the staff became more familiar with the families and families with the staff, the efforts to recruit families to join the school's parent advisory council were highly successful. While understanding a school's culture, let alone an advisory council, can be challenging for the most seasoned parent and educator, it can be particularly challenging for parents of English learners and educators alike, especially when each has no familiarity with the other (Zacarian, 2012). Mrs. Rodrigues was greatly able to support families and educators to work together by first socializing together on behalf of their common investment—the students.

6. **Collaborating with Community:** Coordinate resources and services from the community for families, students, and the school, and provide services to the community.

Sample Practices

- information for students and families on community health, cultural/recreational/ social support, and other programs or services;
- information on community activities that link to learning skills and talents, including summer programs for students;
- service integration through partnerships involving school; civic, counseling, cultural, health, recreation, and other agencies and organizations; and businesses;
- service to the community by students, families, and schools (e.g., recycling, art, music, drama, and other activities for seniors or others); and
- participation of alumni in school programs for students.

  Example: At Wolfe Street Academy in Baltimore, Maryland, many students were in need of dental care. They formed a mutually beneficial partnership with the University of Maryland's School of Dentistry. Under the leadership of the school and its dentistry partner, dental students obtained invaluable experience working with young children and young children received much-needed dental care to address the issues that were significantly impacting their health and well-being (WETA Public Broadcasting, 2019).

The following practical steps, according to Zacarian, Alvarez-Ortiz, and Haynes (2017), are helpful to include in building successful community partnerships:

- Assemble a group of educators and families who
  - understand the strengths and assets of their school and family communities,
  - can identify the needs of the students and families, and
  - are excited to work with a community partner.
- Assign a school–community liaison to identify a community partner that will engage in a mutually beneficial relationship that values the strengths and assets of all students and families.
- Work with an identified community partner to address a school's challenges and strengthen its assets in a mutually beneficial way.

1. **How do the six types of parental involvement assist you in your communication and partnerships with parents?**

   _____

   _____

   _____

   _____

   _____

   _____

2. **Create two examples that describe what you will or would do to include families in classroom decisions (type 5) and coordinate resources from the community (type 6)?**

   _____

   _____

   _____

In our next chapter, we will extend our interactive framework to examine approaches and authentic examples of culturally responsive school-wide practices.

5

Building Culturally Responsive Schools

A HIGH SCHOOL CHEMISTRY TEACHER, Mr. Pratt, describes one of his students passionately. He says, "I heard from Lawrence's previous teacher that I should not be surprised by his being chronically late to my first period class. The teacher also told me that he thought there was 'trouble at home' but that he wasn't too sure what was happening. He said something like, 'Lawrence is a kind but quiet student, and I never quite figured out why he was late so often.'" Hearing this, Mr. Pratt figured that the best thing to do was to see for himself if Lawrence was tardy and, if he was, to ask him about it in a sensitive way that would show him that he cared about him and wanted him to be part of the classroom community. When he noticed that, indeed, Lawrence was late three days in a row, he decided it was the right time to speak with him about it.

Mr. Pratt said, "What would you like me to know about why you are late to class? I miss your coming on time and want to be sure I understand." Lawrence told him that he was responsible for his younger brothers and sisters, including helping them get to school on time. He explained that he made them breakfast, helped them dress, and walked them to school and that these tasks often meant that he was late to school. He went on to explain that his mother had just completed a drug treatment program and was doing her best to resume the morning duties that Lawrence had done while she was in treatment.

Mr. Pratt thanked Lawrence for taking the time to share with him what was occurring. He thought carefully about qualities and attributes that Lawrence possessed either inherently or as a result of the adversity that he had faced. In response, Mr. Pratt stated, "Lawrence, it takes a lot of responsibility on your part to care for your brothers and sisters, to do what you are doing, and it also takes a lot to help your mom in a way that will work well for her. Let's see what we can do to support you to do well in this class."

After the conversation, Mr. Pratt went to speak with Lawrence's English teacher, Ms. Gibbs, and his other teachers to find out what they knew about his student. Ms. Gibbs said, "He's one of those frequent flyers. I never know whether he will show up or not. I have a strong feeling and am worried that he will fail my class. In fact, sadly, I won't be surprised at all and that frustrates me as I don't know what to do. I am glad you are asking me about him. Maybe we could think of ways that you help him." Following this conversation, he spoke with Lawrence's mathematics teacher, Mr. St. Pierre, and found he spoke highly of Lawrence, stating that he participates when called on, turns in his homework faithfully when he comes to class, and that he is a strong math student. His U.S. history teacher, Mr. Reynolds, spoke about Lawrence using the same type of despair as his English teacher—he was sure that Lawrence would fail and expressed concern that "He seems like he's making no effort to learn." Mr. Pratt returned to his classroom more determined to support Lawrence to be successful in his science class.

In this chapter, we move beyond the classroom to the school to describe approaches and some authentic examples of culturally responsive school-wide practices. We begin by revisiting our interactive framework and the contributions of Geneva Gay and others to look more deeply at what we mean by culturally responsive school-wide practices. Before embarking on this journey, let's engage in a reflection activity about the type of interactive exchanges we heard between Mr. Pratt and his colleague, Ms. Gibbs.

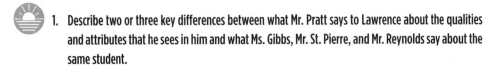

1. Describe two or three key differences between what Mr. Pratt says to Lawrence about the qualities and attributes that he sees in him and what Ms. Gibbs, Mr. St. Pierre, and Mr. Reynolds say about the same student.

   _____

   _____

   _____

2. Think of the types of conversations you have observed about students such as Lawrence. Would they generally seem like Mr. Pratt and Mr. St. Pierre or Mr. Reynolds and Ms. Gibbs? Explain your thoughts and perceptions.

   _____

   _____

   _____

3. Which do you believe provides you with information that sparks your interest in supporting students such as Lawrence, and why?

_____

_____

_____

WHAT DOES IT MEAN TO BE A CULTURALLY RESPONSIVE SCHOOL?

In 2010, Geneva Gay suggested that culturally responsive teaching is important but that it alone cannot solve the major challenges facing students of color. Instead, she reiterated the importance of reforming and transforming all aspects of education, including funding, policymaking, and administration, so they are also culturally responsive. Similarly, scholar Linda Darling-Hammond (2006), renowned for her contributions in educational equity, suggested that every school has its own cultural ways of being that can range in accessibility from those that are welcoming to all to those that are alienating, particularly when it comes to ethnically diverse students. In Darling-Hammond's words:

> "Schools themselves have a culture—a set of norms and ways of working, think-
> ing, talking, valuing, and behaving. When the culture of the school reflects the
> culture of the home or community, the classroom is more familiar to children.
> When school reflects different ways of thinking, knowing, and valuing, children
> must cross boundaries, making the learning process more complex. School can
> be a more foreign experience, and more mysterious or intimidating, for students
> whose home or community context is substantially different from what they
> experience in school. If the school does not incorporate aspects of students'
> home and community life in the learning process, students may feel alienated
> by the classroom environment."

Unfortunately, such transformations and shifts that move a school from alien-ating some to none of its students are yet to happen soundly and consistently from classroom to classroom, school to school, within a district, and district to district. This is particularly true for students who do not represent the dominant population and may feel and be isolated and disconnected from being members of their class-room and school communities. If we look at our focal student, Lawrence, for exam-ple, we see that two of his teachers have completely different perceptions of him. If we are urging teachers to adjust their teaching in ways that respond effectively to children's cultural learning and social needs in the classroom, as Gay and Darling-Hammond suggest, then school leaders must have similar mandates regarding the entire school culture and climate.

According to Vogel (2011), culturally responsive school leaders must also ensure that they hire culturally responsive teachers and encourage them to use culturally responsive pedagogical and classroom management strategies, as well as hold them accountable for doing so. It requires engaging in several key conditions:

- self-reflection;
- examining implicit bias;
- exploring microaggressions, including microassaults, microinsults, and micro-invalidations, and taking steps to address them;
- embracing collaborative reflection;
- creating a mistake-safe, culturally responsive school;
- applying excellence through an equity lens; and
- using a culturally responsive scorecard tool.

SELF-REFLECTION

Gay and Kirkland (2003) suggest that to move a school toward culturally responsive leadership, there must first be a process of critical self-reflection, where leaders understand their own multiple identities before they can build cultural responsiveness within their teachers and staff. This is a critically important stance. Ijeoma Oluo (2017), a best-selling author about race relations, talks about why it is challenging and, at the same time, critically important for people to take time to examine their feelings and perceptions on what they say and do—especially as it relates to interactional patterns of oppressing others. The type of self-reflection that she is encouraging can occur by taking time to understand the types of stereotypes and biases that we hold and how they seep into all that we think, do, and say on a daily basis.

An example of the type of stereotypes and deficit-based assumptions that we are referring to is a White teacher who learns that she will have a student who is "known for picking fights with others." When the student arrives and is seen to be a person of color, the same teacher can unconsciously or consciously add deficit-based assumptions about the student, such as "Students from *that* neighborhood are from a gang." Having thoughts and perceptions such as these can and do result in perpetuating these deficit-based assumptions and beliefs in ways that further hinder and, indeed, damage our capacity to support such students in school and out of school.

Engaging in the type of practices that Gay and Kirkland as well as Oluo refer to also call for school leaders and others engaging in hiring practices (e.g., human resource staff, school teams, and/or district teams) to secure candidates that are the most likely to engage in the type of self-reflection to which we are referring. An example is Ms. Gibbs, the English teacher of our focal student, Lawrence. Ms. Gibbs is in her first year of teaching. During her interview, she and another candidate were asked to describe an example of a culturally responsive practice. Ms. Gibbs shared a very powerful example of a student whose parents lost their jobs and spent part of the year in a homeless shelter. In describing the student, she discussed her student's commitment to school, his passion for learning, and his dedication to stay after school to try and make up the work that he missed while his family was living in a car. Let's also say that she continued her response to include, "I am always seeking ways to support my students to do well, even when some face obstacles and challenges that might seem impossible. Also, I am grateful to have colleagues to support me in this work." Though a new teacher, Ms. Gibbs speaks to a key feature of culturally responsive schools: they routinely engage in individual and group reflection and have a collaborative spirit.

EXAMINING IMPLICIT BIAS

Oluo (2017) also discusses the critical importance of understanding implicit bias: "I don't want you to understand me better, I want you to understand yourselves. Your survival has never depended on your knowledge of White culture. In fact, it has required your ignorance." The teaching profession has not traditionally applied Oluo's ideas as a first step. As educators, the majority of our professional development and professionalism has depended on our doing our best to understand our students and their needs and adapt the curriculum so that we can connect it as seamlessly and successfully as possible to our students' personal, social, academic, and life experiences. Whether we are referring to academic or social-emotional learning, and while educators must be prepared to understand their students and build instructional programming based on this knowledge, the essential first step that Oluo is demanding is self-awareness of our own culture and biases. It is only by understanding and reflecting on our own biases (and we all have inherent biases due to our experiences and upbringings) that we can begin to make changes in our mindsets, pedagogy, and management choices. An article written in *Education Week* (Schwartz, 2019), entitled "Next Step in Diversity Training: Teachers Learn to Face Their Unconscious Biases," provides guidance regarding systemic approaches to implicit bias training.

In the same *Education Week* article (Schwartz, 2019), Kathleen King Thorius, executive director of the Great Lakes Equity Center in Indianapolis was interviewed and stated, "Historically, teacher diversity trainings have been focused on understanding the behavior or characteristics of students who come from different backgrounds than their teachers. Implicit bias and equity training flip this script. It requires teachers to critically examine how their own identities have shaped their experiences. And it proposes a call to action: 'What should we, as teachers, do about inequities?'" One of the school districts featured in the *Education Week* article was Long Beach Unified School District in California, where teachers are working with a youth advocacy organization called Californians for Justice on implicit bias and relationship-centered schools.

EXPLORING MICROAGGRESSIONS

Similarly, micro-aggressions, or "everyday insults, indignities and demeaning messages sent to people of color by well-intentioned white people who are unaware of the hidden messages being sent to them" can also oftentimes occur in the classroom setting (Sue, 2007). The term *racial microaggressions* was first proposed by psychiatrist Chester M. Pierce, MD, in the 1970s, but psychologists have significantly elaborated on the concept in recent years. In his landmark work on stereotype threat, for instance, Stanford University psychology professor Claude Steele, PhD, has shown that African Americans and women perform worse on academic tests when aware of stereotypes about race or gender (2011). Women who were primed with stereotypes about women's poor math performance do worse on math tests. Blacks' intelligence test scores plunge when they're primed with stereotypes about Blacks' inferior intelligence. In this way, Steele defines stereotype threat as, ". . . being at risk of confirming, as a self-characteristic, a negative stereotype about one's social group" (Steele & Aronson, 1995). As educators, we must recognize how we contribute to manifestations of stereotype threat within ourselves and our students. Similarly, we must assist our students with being aware of, and then rejecting, negative messages about their social group, and replacing them with positive messages about their identities.

One way of combatting stereotype threats is by being aware of racial microaggressions and how they can manifest themselves in the classroom setting. Sue first proposed a classification of racial microaggressions in a 2007 article on how they manifest in clinical practice in the *American Psychologist* (Vol. 2, No. 4). He notes three types of current racial microaggressions:

- *Microassaults*: Conscious and intentional actions or slurs, such as using racial epithets, displaying swastikas, or deliberately serving a White person before a person of color in a restaurant.
  - In the classroom setting, this can include overly calling on White students and ignoring or not calling on students of color.

- *Microinsults*: Verbal and nonverbal communications that subtly convey rudeness and insensitivity and demean a person's racial heritage or identity. An example is an employee who asks a colleague of color how she got her job, implying she may have landed it through an affirmative action or quota system.
    - In the classroom setting, this can mean questioning female students or students of color who are in AP courses or who have earned good grades.
- *Microinvalidations*: Communications that subtly exclude, negate, or nullify the thoughts, feelings, or experiential reality of a person of color. For instance, White people often ask Asian Americans where they were born, conveying the message that they are perpetual foreigners in their own land.
    - In the classroom setting, this can mean making assumptions about students' lack of background experiences, including assuming that ELs haven't traveled or are not "cultured."

Sue focuses on microinsults and microinvalidations because of their less obvious nature, which puts people of color in a psychological bind. He suggests, "While the person may feel insulted, she is not sure exactly why, and the perpetrator doesn't acknowledge that anything has happened because he is not aware that he has been offensive." As teachers, then, we must become aware of how to address microinsults and microinvalidations when they manifest themselves in the classroom setting. This begins by becoming aware of our blind spots and implicit biases, as well as having the courage to advocate for *all* of our students.

1. What kinds of stereotype threats have you personally experienced or internalized?

_____

_____

_____

2. How can you assist students with undoing stereotype threats they may have internalized?

_____

_____

_____

3. What can you do in a classroom setting to combat microassaults, microinvalidations, and microinsults?

_____

_____

_____

4. Has any of your own professional growth included implicit bias training? If not, develop a plan to learn more about implicit bias.

_____

_____

_____

EMBRACING COLLABORATIVE REFLECTION

What is also needed to do our best *for* our students is understanding deeply what it means to be an educator in a professional culture in which the majority of us hail from a White-dominant experience as opposed to the growing number of diverse students with whom we most need to reach. Oluo argues adeptly that what is essential is our taking time to understand what it means to be a member of this culture so that we can more readily understand the differences or multiple identities that present themselves in our students, their families, and the communities in which they live. Further, this type of exploration can only occur successfully when it is a group effort in which everyone is willing to look closely at the culture in which our students learn from us and we take seriously what it means to be wholly culturally responsible systemically and institutionally as opposed to partially culturally responsible.

An example is Mr. Pratt, the focal teacher introduced at the beginning of this chapter and his efforts to seek information from colleagues about his student Lawrence. Figure 5.1 describes the various perceptions that Lawrence's mathematics, U.S. History, and English teachers shared with his science teacher. They have been separated to include language that describes Lawrence using asset-based and deficit-based language.

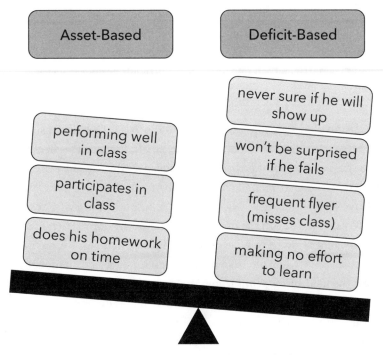

Figure 5.1: Teachers' Perceptions of Lawrence's Attributes and Characteristics

Reread the third paragraph of this chapter where Mr. Pratt tells Lawrence the characteristics and attributes that he sees in him. Using Figure 5.1, add these statements to the columns (asset-based or deficit-based) that you believe are the best fit.

Using the information you just added, how might you support a group of educators to perceive Lawrence in the best light possible? _____

_____

_____

_____

Often times when we interview individuals about their passion for the work of being an educator, they describe the elements that continuously drive their motivation to teach. The types of responses we receive replicate what has been written by others. For example, in 2005, scholar in social justice Sonia Nieto edited a book titled *Why We Teach* (Dunn, 2005). It included a series of essays written by teachers from the field. One of the contributors was Bill Dunn. Here are a few of the gems he had to share about why he chose teaching as a profession:

"I teach because someone has to tell my students that they are not the ones who are dumb. . . . I teach because my students need to know that poverty does not equal stupidity. I teach because my students need to know that surviving a bleak and dismal childhood makes you strong and tough and beautiful in ways that only survivors of similar environments can appreciate and understand. I teach because my students need to know that in their struggle to acquire a second language, they participate in one of the most difficult human feats . . ." *(Dunn, 2005, p. 180)*

Though Dunn died suddenly at the age of 59 in 2011, he was considered a social justice advocate by his local newspaper (Nieto, 2014). Perhaps this occurred because he was more than willing to bravely and courageously discuss the positive and powerful visions of equity that he had for his students. In 2014, 10 years after the first series of essays were published, Nieto edited a second newer and fresher version titled, *Why We Teach Now.* In the opening chapter of the book, Nieto calls for teachers to be trusted and allowed to have an active and participatory voice in discussing, sharing, and collectively learning from their views, concerns, challenges, and aspirations about the field of teaching to make improvements and adjustments to what they do. With all of the testing and accountability mandates, coupled with all of the changes to our student and family populations that are occurring or will occur, we should all be championing the call to support teachers to have more of a say.

To realize the battle cry requires school leaders in rural, suburban, and urban settings to support those who teach as well as every member of the school community to feel safe, a sense of belonging to the school community, valued, and competent (Zacarian, Alvarez-Ortiz, & Haynes, 2017). These four essential conditions require school leaders to create and embrace a mistake-safe, culturally responsive school.

CREATING A MISTAKE-SAFE, CULTURALLY RESPONSIVE SCHOOL

Part of our challenge in creating culturally responsive schools is to support the goodness and capacities that all students possess so that they may put forth their best efforts and aspirations. If we revisit Figure 5.1, one of the most important efforts we must engage in is examining our individual and collective perceptions of students as well as their families. To do this wholeheartedly, school leaders must know how and when to offer support or correction and when to step back and allow a school community of educators to make adjustments on their own or with peers (Zacarian & Silverstone, 2020). A second and no less important challenge is for leaders to know how to support a school-wide and even district-wide collective reflection so that everyone in the community, including its leaders, are willing to learn from mistakes and perceptions openly, trustingly, and safely without being fearful of embarrassment, losing face, or judgment.

This challenge calls for creating an environment of cultural responsiveness in which educators can have candid discussions of concerns and errors so that we may individually and collectively be much more conscious of how to create a mistake-safe culture in which we are more willing to learn from our errors than cover them up or brush them aside for fear of embarrassment or failure (Zacarian & Silverstone, 2020). It calls for the type of self- and collaborative reflection we have stated is needed for educators to know themselves and be aware of their implicit biases and microaggressions so that they don't repeat them. An example of the mistake-safe, school-wide cultural practice that we are advocating for comes from the medical field. Researcher Edmonson (2004) examined the social psychology of errors and accidents in hospital settings. He found that the two primary catalysts for a group's willingness to explore and understand its errors and accidents were:

1. Being a member of a culture that openly and honestly talks about concerns, fears, and errors so that everyone is much more consciously and continuously aware of how to reduce these.
2. Leaders foster an environment that is safe and nurturing especially for analyzing the environment's challenges, pitfalls, and successes.

An additional or third element of a mistake-safe, culturally responsive culture is also one in which:

3. Everyone in the school community sees themselves as willing to humbly grow and change to meet the ever-changing needs of their student and family populations. This process takes humility on the part of all participants but particularly and most importantly those in the dominant culture who might find themselves believing that they have all of the answers and are not used to taking a humble stance.

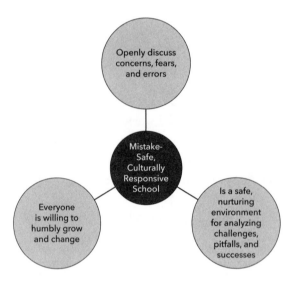

Figure 5.2: Mistake-Safe Responsive Culture

An example of the type of mistake-safe, culturally responsive culture is the school that Lawrence attends. Rather than Mr. Pratt feeling alone in his quest to support Lawrence, he attends staff meetings where strategies in Figures 5.1 and 5.2 are routinely utilized, in words, deeds, and actions, to support everyone to think more proactively about the ways in which the school community can be much more aware of new ways to show its changing student population they are cared for and about. For example, in Figure 5.1, we can readily see that a hefty amount of deficit-based language is being used to describe our focal student, Lawrence, that it is tipping the scale to the deficit side. Rather than pummel educators figuratively for their negative views, school leaders must use these moments to examine educators' feelings and perceptions in ways that will support them to know that they are secure, valued, and competent, all the while pushing for students to receive a positively powerful, successful experience.

A mistake-safe culture calls for us to look at equity in ways that allow for flexibility in creating an environment that has the most likelihood to work for each of our students to be the best versions of themselves. For example, Lawrence is chronically late and, given his home circumstances, his tardiness is likely to continue.

A hallmark of a mistake-safe responsive culture is that we have to recognize the messiness of finding solutions, that everyone makes mistakes, that the credo—*two steps forward, one step back*—has meaning in schools. Rather than expect perfection, we should strive for growth through collective reflection so that we can be and are prepared to learn from, grow from, and grow with each other. In other words, adaptations and responses to what we collectively believe must occur does not happen by the snap of a finger. They happen when we are willing to try new ideas on and see which ones fit the best as we undertake the craft of teaching. They also happen when we collectively understand differences as distinctions for growth instead of barriers and impossible obstacles to growth.

An example of this is the teacher who is bilingual bicultural and can easily understand the lives of his students *because* he has been immersed in the same way of being and acting as them since birth. That reality does not mean that another teacher who is not bilingual bicultural cannot reach students in a positive and affirmational way. It means that each of us must take time to work together on behalf of our students. As Karen Beeman (2012), co-author of *Teaching for Biliteracy,* suggests, "You do not need to be bilingual to employ a multilingual/growth mindset. You need to be open to the mindset." And, most importantly, this can only occur when we are continuously encouraged to do so by leaders who consistently encourage this type of professional growth. Leaders such as this understand that the process of growth is not linear; it involves the messiness of trying things out to see what fits by being and consistently encouraging openness and flexibility. Ultimately, however, leaders and educators alike must understand and continually be in a learning stance when it comes to systemic racism. As Robin DiAngelo (2018) suggests in her *New York Times* bestselling book, *White Fragility: Why It's So Hard for White People to Talk about Racism,* "Racism is a system, not an event. We either participate in or disrupt racism. It takes effort not to know. Break the apathy. It's on me to continually educate myself about racism."

 1. **What adaptations do you believe might be made to successfully accommodate Lawrence's and his family's (including his younger siblings) needs without compromising his performance in this subject matter or his matriculation at school?**

_____

_____

_____

2. What can you do to begin to disrupt racism at school or within a classroom setting?

_____

_____

_____

3. What kind of professional development plan can you create to continually educate yourself about systemic racism?

_____

_____

_____

APPLYING EXCELLENCE THROUGH AN EQUITY LENS

According to sociologist Pedro Noguera and educator Alan Blankstein (2016), educators should ensure the conditions needed for good teaching and learning by including equitable learning environments, where students receive what they need academically and socially. Our focal student, Lawrence, is an example for discussing the differences that can and do occur among our student populations. In his case, he is often late or absent from school. Figure 5.3 describes his school's code of conduct policies for being absent from or tardy to school as well as the reasons Lawrence is tardy or absent. Let's look closely at our thinking about cultural responsiveness; particularly as it relates to the following the foundational precepts of culturally responsive education:

1. Honor, value, and acknowledge students' various identities, values, and life experiences.
2. Disrupt power imbalances to create equity and excellence.
3. Empower students.

Our focal student, Lawrence, is certainly doing his best to support his family and attend school. When he is absent or tardy, he is engaging in actions to provide much-needed support to his family. His actions call for us to do our best to create policies and actions that in which we, as educators, engage in:

- Creating a match between the needs of the students and the skills of the staff to meet those needs, including a holistic educational approach and the ability to provide differentiated support. Staff must be able to assist students in understanding and responding to their environments.

Figure 5.3: Code of Conduct Policies at Lawrence's School—Absences and Tardies

Code of Conduct	Lawrence
ABSENCES A student who is absent at least one half of a class period shall be counted as absent from that class. EXCUSED ABSENCES Students must be in school unless the absence has been permitted or excused for one of the following reasons. • A student is ill or injured. • There is a major illness in the student's immediate family (this means parents, brothers, sisters, grandparents, or others living in the home). • There is a death in the immediate family. • The student has a scheduled medical or dental appointment. • There is a religious holiday in the student's own faith. • The student is required by summons, subpoena or court order to appear in court. A copy of the subpoena or court order must be given to the principal. • There is a 'special event' such as a conference, activity, etc. which requires being absent from school. The student must receive permission from the principal at least five days prior to the absence. • The student is excused from school due to an illness such as lice or other communicable challenges which requires his/her absence. UNEXCUSED ABSENCES Any absence which does not meet the criteria stated of an excused absence is an unexcused absence. TARDIES A student is tardy when the student is not in his or her assigned seat when the bell rings. EXCUSED TARDY A tardy is excused only if the student is late for one of the reasons described in the section labeled 'excused absence.'	Mother just completed drug treatment program. Lawrence helps his younger siblings get to school on time. He makes them breakfast, helps them dress, and walks them to school—resulting in his chronic tardiness. If a sibling misses school for one of the reasons listed, Lawrence cares for him/her.

- Understanding the lives of students outside of school, including how they learn inside of school, their motive and interests, and the challenges of the family and unmet needs.
- Providing supports and services that revolve around the needs of the students served, including parent-community ties, student-centered learning environment, and a shared leadership to drive change.
- Applying a sense of urgency to address disparities in achievement, which includes a paradigm shift in ability, the role of the school to develop students, resources allocated according to student need, and discipline that reinforces school values.

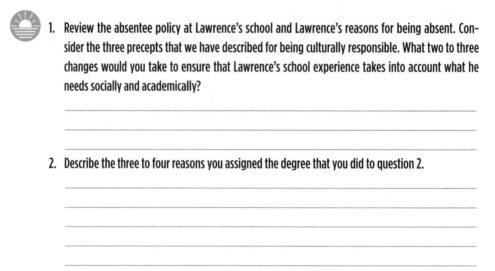

1. Review the absentee policy at Lawrence's school and Lawrence's reasons for being absent. Consider the three precepts that we have described for being culturally responsible. What two to three changes would you take to ensure that Lawrence's school experience takes into account what he needs socially and academically?

_____

_____

_____

2. Describe the three to four reasons you assigned the degree that you did to question 2.

_____

_____

_____

_____

_____

According to Noguera (2016), a vision for pursuing excellence through equity should take into account: teaching and learning, extended learning, safety/mentors, community partnerships with universities and other institutions, family engagement, and health and nutrition. While we will discuss community partners in our next chapter, it is important to state here that many schools, including the school that our focal student Lawrence attends, should not expect to have all the answers. However, it is critical that we not embark on the work of building culturally responsive leadership or schools alone as one person or even a small team of people do not have and should not think they have all of the answers. Rather, when we partner with students, families, our school and district community, and the local and even broader community, we have a much better opportunity to support students to be successful in school and in their lives.

APPLYING A CULTURALLY RESPONSIVE SCORECARD

A very helpful tool that school leaders and teachers might consider using to analyze their curriculum and determine the degree that it is culturally responsive is The Metropolitan Center for Research on Equity and Transformation of Schools Culturally Responsive Curriculum (CRC) Scorecard (2019), developed by New York University's Education Justice Research and Organizing Collaborative. It was designed with K–8 English Language Arts textbooks in mind but is applicable to other grades and subjects. A key aspect of the tool is its grounding in cultural responsive practices by ensuring that it is infused with "stories, activities, assignments, and illustrations that influence how young people understand the world and contribute to centering and normalizing people, cultures and values" (p. 4). The overarching goal of the CRC Scorecard is twofold and includes a means for:

1. describing and critiquing culturally destructive curriculum; and
2. imagining and describing intersectional and critical, culturally responsive curriculum; it was much easier to talk about what culturally responsive curriculum was *not* than to talk about what it *was*, because there are so many examples of problematic curricula.

According to the website where the CRC Scorecard can be downloaded (https://steinhardt.nyu.edu/metrocenter/resources/culturally-responsive-scorecard), the best way to use the tool is to assemble a diverse evaluation team, follow the CRC Scorecard Guidelines, and complete seven steps to determine the extent to which a school has culturally responsive curriculum. Briefly, the seven steps include:

1. Getting a copy of the child's/school's curriculum
2. Selecting a curriculum evaluation team that has at least three people of diverse races, genders, ages, sexuality, classes, national origins and roles (parent, student, teacher, administrator, community member)
3. Choosing grades, units, and lessons to analyze
4. Pulling out keywords to view
5. Conducting the evaluation using the scorecard
6. Scoring the evaluation
7. Discussing findings with the team (p. 5)

Further, the Scorecard was also designed to be "customized to the context and conditions" of each school district . . . (p. 5). With this in mind, let's return to our focal student, Lawrence, and the team that his school principal has assembled. The principal wants to create an eight-person interdisciplinary team made up of English language arts, U.S. history, special education, and English as a second language teachers and a student and family member. He also wants it to include diverse-aged adults, so he selects his youngest staff member, Ms. Gibbs, to represent English language arts and his oldest staff member, Mr. Reynolds, to represent the U.S. history department. Both are the two teachers who lamented Lawrence's lack of success in school. Knowing that Lawrence has missed a good deal of school and is at risk of failing, the principal also asks him to be a member of the team for two reasons: (1) to support his becoming a stronger member of the school community and (2) to support the school in being more culturally responsive.

As the group engages in its task, both Ms. Gibbs and Mr. Reynolds begin to question the school's curriculum capacity to be the most responsive to its diverse student populations. For example, Ms. Gibbs notes that few pieces of literature that are used are actually written about diverse experiences or by diverse authors. As they learn more about Lawrence's home experience, they also begin to question their school's attendance policies to take into account the growing number of students, such as Lawrence, who experience adversity. Based on this information as well as additional information they gain as a result of their evaluation, they begin to list the steps they can and will take to ensure that the school's policies, curriculum, and materials used to teach are more of a match to its student and family populations.

1. Go to pages 6–7 of the Scorecard and review three sections: representation, social justice, and teacher's materials. As you read about model schools and the highest ratings in the sections that follow, determine the degree to which your work context is truly culturally responsible.

   _____

   _____

   _____

   _____

   _____

2. How do you see yourself using the CRC Scorecard at your school site during department or grade-level meetings?

   _____

   _____

   _____

   _____

A CULTURALLY RESPONSIVE SCHOOL MODEL

As we have suggested in other chapters, an increasing body of research demonstrates the importance of addressing the needs of culturally and linguistically diverse students and their families. Unfortunately, the cultural underpinning of schools in the United States is largely still consistent with middle-class, European values (Boykin, 1994), leading many schools to ignore or downplay the strengths of diverse students and their families. This may be occurring as the majority of educators are White (U.S. Department of Education, 2016) or White and middle class (Hollins & Guzman, 2005). Seminal research completed by Valenzuela (1999) on Mexican American high school students defined this approach as subtractive schooling. An example of subtractive schooling is when schools ignored students' knowledge of Spanish or even treated it as a deficit.

With this as a backdrop, it is essential to note the groundbreaking research that identified ways in which schools *can* serve students of color effectively. For example, renowned seminal studies of the Advancement Via Individual Determination (AVID) college and career preparation program in San Diego, California, demonstrated the importance of high expectations versus tracking ethnic and language-minority students into low-level classes (Mehan, Villanueva, Hubbard, & Lintz, 1996). Setting high expectations and providing a "scaffold" of support greatly helped (and continues to help) students of color succeed. AVID gives students direct instruction in the "hidden curriculum" of the school—which courses to take, which teachers to seek out, the importance of tests, and how to study. Although AVID students oftentimes demonstrate positive results, it is rare to find schools that have utilized these scaffolds and strategies for students of color *schoolwide*. However, there are school-wide approaches that are important to consider because they have created culturally responsive practices from their inception. In this section, we will further highlight the previously mentioned Roses in Concrete in Oakland, California, as it embodies the type of promising practices that undergird our conception of culturally responsive schools.

Roses in Concrete Community Charter School

In 2015, Roses in Concrete Community School, a K–8 charter school, opened in East Oakland, California. The school aims to create a model for urban education that prioritizes the needs of youth and families in the community it serves. The name of the Roses in Concrete Community School was inspired by the book of poetry based on the writings of Tupac Shakur released in 1999, *The Rose That Grew from Concrete*.

As the school website suggests, "The vivid image [of the rose in concrete] captures the need to celebrate the tenacity and will of the rose against-all-odds, finds a way to grow in the inhospitable and toxic environment of the concrete that it might transform the concrete into a rose again." Its founder, Dr. Jeff Duncan-Andrade, who is also an associate professor of Latina/Latino studies and education administration and interdisciplinary studies at San Francisco State University, believes, as we do, that education is *the* way to help young people understand they can transform not only their community but also the world.

Duncan-Andrade designed the school so that students receive an individualized approach to education. His goal and the goal of the school is to recognize and consider each student as their own person with their own needs, their own abilities that can be utilized, and their own voice that needs to be heard. He believes in the wrap-around approach in education, which is practiced at Roses because "no child can learn in a classroom if they're hungry, unsafe, or unhappy with themselves." Under the community school approach and Duncan-Andrade's vision, the school takes the needs of the community into consideration when mapping out its pedagogical methods, which are culturally relevant and responsive.

For example, in the school's first year, Google provided $750,000 to help launch Roses in Concrete's unique vision. Google then awarded an additional $650,000 grant to help the school build a first-of-its-kind computer science (CS) curriculum to serve as a model for other schools across the U.S. The curriculum is culturally and community relevant, building on Duncan-Andrade's philosophy that education shouldn't push students out of communities, but should instead help students transform them. Additionally, the school has developed a dual immersion strand within the school, in order to validate the languages that students bring with them from home.

The Roses in Concrete school is also designed to serve as an apprenticeship pipeline to train skilled teachers who will go on to work in Oakland public schools, bringing an understanding of this philosophy with them. Duncan-Andrade recruits talented educators from around the country who will mentor undergraduates at San Francisco State, Mills College, Stanford University, and other Bay Area institutions. In personal correspondence with Duncan-Andrade (2019), he stated, "We will be literally growing our own for the district. Teachers need to reclaim what good teaching is. Part of the goal is to really study what the most effective teachers do and how they do it, to use the tools of research on a much deeper level." In addition to the teacher apprenticeship program, Duncan-Andrade describes the school as an open lab for the practice of teaching and better understanding how successful strategies can be replicated.

1. What stood out for you about Roses in Concrete Community School?

_____

_____

_____

2. What elements of this school might you want to be sure are incorporated into your own classroom and school?

_____

_____

_____

In our next chapter, we will move beyond the school to the ways schools can create comprehensive and sustained partnerships with local community members, agencies, and civic and business organizations that are built from our culturally responsive framework.

6

Building Culturally Responsive School–Community Connections

DR. CLEMENCIA VARGAS, from the University of Maryland School of Dentistry, describes the reciprocal partnership that has been forged with Wolfe Street School in Baltimore, Maryland. An important feature of the partnership is to honor and value families—many of whom are from Latin America. She describes what she knows to be important to families:

> "There are a variety of beliefs about teeth in Latin America, about how long to breastfeed, for example, or what type of food to give [a] child. So, we work within those parameters. We are not coming to the community and say[ing], this is how you do it, and this is how it has to be done. We start with what the parents need, what the parents want to learn, and we use also – that brings me to the technique we use. We use motivational interviews in our activities, so we start with where the parent is in oral health, what they know, what they need to know, what they want to know more, what changes they are ready to make."
> *(Dr. Clemencia Vargas, University of Maryland School of Dentistry, 2019)*

In this chapter, we move beyond the school to the community to discuss the importance of creating active partnerships between a school or district and local community members, agencies, and civic and business organizations using our culturally responsive framework. The partnership between the University of Maryland School of Dentistry and Wolfe Street Academy (described in the quote at the opening of this chapter) ensured that the students at Wolfe Street Academy received much needed dental care. Ninety-six percent of the students at Wolfe Street Academy receive free/reduced lunch (IEL, 2015) and many had not had prior dental care and were coming to school in pain (Vargas, 2019). In 2015, according to the Institute for Educational Leadership (IEL, 2015), Wolfe Street "moved from the 77th to the 2nd highest performing school in Baltimore since adopting a community schools' strategy nine years ago." This outcome speaks to the positive outcomes that can occur through building culturally responsive school–community partnerships.

WHY ENGAGE IN COMMUNITY PARTNERSHIPS?

Thus far in our book, our interactive framework has included students, their families, and members of a school community. Indeed, in Chapter 2, we introduced these as the circles of interactions (Zacarian & Silverstone, 2015; Zacarian, Alvarez-Ortiz, & Haynes, 2017) that students engage in (see Figure 2.1 in Chapter 2) and repeat it here in Figure 6.1.

The diversity of a local community or even a global community is an integral component of our circles of interaction framework. There are many reasons for these outermost circles. School–community partnerships, that is partnerships with

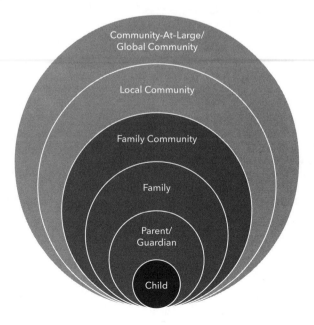

Figure 6.1: Circles of Interactions

local community-based individuals, agencies, organizations, and institutions as well as the broader community, provide us with invaluable resources. Left untapped, schools and districts would rapidly become a completely separate and marginalized entity *from* the community. Further, the absence of these crucial partnerships leads to a school district being what family–school partnership experts Henderson, Mapp, Johnson and Davies (2007) call an isolated *fortress*. Unfortunately, such isolation often leads to students greatly missing out on the positive possibilities that can and do occur when members of the community partner with their local school and/or district on behalf of students' engagement, academic success, and active participatory membership in their local school, community, and beyond. For example, consider a student who has not had access to dental care and comes to school in significant pain from a toothache.

Studies by Mapp et al. (2007) and Epstein (2011) show a deep connection between school–community partnerships and students' well-being as well as the gains made to support enduring learning and 21st-century goals. With all of these positives about the efficacy of school–community partnerships, it is as important that they address the identified needs or assets of its students, particularly, as we will discuss in this chapter, those from culturally and linguistically diverse experiences. Further, the partnership requires leaders to actively support working with community partners on behalf of students' success. Educational leader and writer Paul Houston (2011) calls for the type of leadership that embraces and wholeheartedly supports community members in engaging its students in ways that might not otherwise happen. Further, he calls for leaders to look deeply at the possibilities that can and do occur when we partner with others to make learning meaningful, engaging, and compelling for students.

Like Mapp et al., (2011), Houston argues against creating a *fortress school* and foregoing the possibilities of forging partnerships for fear of losing control. He also reminds us that schools are located in the community and, by geographic location alone, are and must be an integral part of the community. Calling upon the well-known African proverb, "It takes a village to raise a child," he calls for the community to be actively engaged with the school for the betterment of its students and the community itself. An important additional point that he makes is the reality that only 30% of a local community has school-age children. As such, it is critical for schools to reach out to and involve all of its citizens so that children become everyone's responsibility. The fruits of this type of labor are well worth the effort.

An example of this is the discussion that Dr. Vargas had about the mutual value of partnerships. While Wolfe Street provides the students with the necessary dental care through its partnership with the University of Maryland School of Dentistry, the University's dental students receive practical experience:

"Dental students come here, and I think probably you saw them sitting down this morning. They're quiet. They haven't—this group hadn't come to work before, and when they started working with the children, they change. They see the children in a very different light. We are talking about pediatric dentistry." *(Vargas, 2019)*

Further, their partnership continues to evolve in mutually beneficial ways. An example that Dr. Vargas shared is the opportunity for dental students to work with parents.

" . . . And every time that we have students interested in doing education with Latino parents, we come here . . . Usually the parents come to [Wolfe Street Academy]—for breakfast . . . So that's a great opportunity just to chat with the parents after the kids have gone to class, and that has worked really well." *(Vargas, 2019)*

This outcome is perhaps one of the greatest (and perhaps most hidden) assets of school–community partnerships—its invaluable capacity to mutually benefit a school, its partner, and the community. In other words, a successful community-school partnership is one that benefits all participants in recognizable and identifiable ways.

1. Describe a mutually beneficial school–community partnership you have engaged or would like to engage in.

   _____

   _____

   _____

2. Describe at least one way the partnership benefitted or could benefit each of the partners in tangible and recognizable ways.

   _____

   _____

   _____

WHAT ARE COMMUNITY SCHOOLS?

Community involvement has been occurring for many years in schools across the nation. However, what has changed or evolved over time are the approaches we use to involve our local community in a more evidence-based and strengths-based way to benefit our ever-increasing, dynamically diverse student and family populations and our communities. This community involvement replicates some of the more contemporary applications of an approach known as *community schools*, whereby partners *come to* the school community.

While one definition of community schools is those "who offer courses to the community and bring community resources into the school" (Houston, 2011, p. 133), many school-based and district-based examples of community schools have broadened or customized it to fit their particular, unique needs in many important and effective ways. Included among these are schools that offer after- and before-school programming as well as medical and dental services. Additionally, there are others who provide a range of community-based college and university partnerships that offer high school students for-credit college courses while obtaining a high school diploma, a combined associate's degree and high school diploma, and more. Each of these examples shows the various possibilities of school–community partnerships in an ever-expanding definition of a community school. We subscribe to the following definition: A school that works as a mutually beneficial partner with the local community.

Three key elements of school–community partnerships are that they require each district or school to:

1. identify a need and/or an asset that would benefit from a community partner;
2. identify local resources that will address the needs/assets; and
3. take steps to create partnerships that are mutually beneficial and as enduring as they are transformative.

Let's look more closely at these three elements by looking at what is involved in creating a culturally responsive school–community approach.

CREATING A CULTURALLY RESPONSIVE SCHOOL–COMMUNITY APPROACH

To support all students to feel secure in knowing that they are valuable contributing members, and that they are treasured for their many competencies in their school and local community, we must have a comprehensive understanding of what it means to be a member—a real member—of a classroom, school, and local community. Many organizations believe this can only occur when educators and communities carefully take time and actions to ensure that all children are "healthy, safe, engaged, supported, and challenged" and refer to this as taking a *whole community, whole school, whole child approach* (ASCD, 2019, para. 2). We believe these conditions are as much a social-emotional as a physical state of well-being. Further, they can only occur when everyone is involved in ensuring that they occur—that is, when families, educators, policymakers, and other stakeholders work steadfastly as dedicated and committed partners on behalf of all students, including the ones we most want to reach.

An example of the type of leadership and school–community partnership we are describing is occurring in Dearborn, Michigan. Sue Stanley is the principal of Salina Elementary School, a PreK–3 school of about 400 children. She recounted her entrée into the position and the steps she took to become familiar with the school, the local community, and the partnerships it had established with the community prior to her tenure. One of the community-based partnerships she described is with her district's superintendent, principals, a representative of the Arab Community Center for Economic and Social Service [ACCESS], and other community stakeholders.

"I replaced a highly respected and loved elementary principal. She retired after many, many years in the district. She was an Arab-American woman who knew the community and was fluent in speaking and writing Arabic. Our population is 98% Yemeni and over 94% EL (English learners). Most of our parents do not speak English. I am a white woman from Italian and Scottish descent. I knew little about the community and their culture. Truth be known, I was pretty worried about how this would all work.

I was hired in late May, so I knew I had a few months to begin getting to know the community before the new school year started. I met with a community group (superintendent and other principals, someone from ACCESS to help be the voice of newcomer parents, and other stakeholders to get to know them). Looking back, I believe my reaching out first made a big difference.

I invited staff to meet with me and held a 'popsicles with the principal' event on the playground a month prior to school starting.

I also spent a lot of time out in the community trying to learn as much as possible about the lives of the students at Salina.

When school started, I continued Friday morning meetings with parents. While we would talk about educational issues, I spent a lot of time asking them questions.

I also began a 'bedtime stories with Mrs. Stanley.' I go into their homes (by invitation only), read them the book and leave it with them. I continue that today and it is one of my most rewarding experiences." *(Stanley, July 25, 2019, personal communication)*

1. Describe three to four different steps that Principal Sue Stanley took to become familiar with the elementary school and local community she serves.

_____

_____

_____

_____

2. How did the steps she took support a whole school, whole community, whole child approach?

_____

_____

_____

Principal Stanley also discusses the importance of empowering teachers.

> "This staff is outstanding. They are the pulse which sets this school aside from others. They epitomize the word 'teacher.' I see my role as making sure they are empowered, appreciated and have everything they need to do their job as they are the most impactful person in the building." *(Stanley, July 29, 2019)*

In addition, she knows the critical value of having staff who represent the cultural and linguistic diversity of its students. In her school, for example, the accounting secretary and parent liaison are bilingual and bicultural members of the Yemeni community and are "firmly rooted in taking care of the community" (Stanley, July 29, 2019, personal communication). Their expertise and depth of understanding about the various ways of being and acting of their student and family populations is invaluable. The school is far better able to identify the needs and assets of its Yemeni community and enact practices that are culturally responsive. Their expertise also allows for recruiting and engaging community partners that can respond to the needs and assets of its learners. For example, the ACCESS partners have been instrumental in supporting the students and families at Salina Elementary School. Principal Stanley shares some of the supports that they have helped to provide.

> "They [ACCESS] are continually looking for grants to support our needs based on our discussions. They have been able to secure grants to provide after-school tutoring and a mental health professional housed in our building one day per week." *(Stanley, July 25, 2019)*

A key element for engaging a partner is to identify a need or an asset that would benefit from a community partner. It is here that we now turn.

IDENTIFYING A NEED OR AN ASSET THAT WOULD BENEFIT FROM A COMMUNITY PARTNER

To create the types of partnerships that work for all students involves taking time to engage in a comprehensive analysis of the various aspects of a child's development in our particular geographic location. Our circles of interactions framework infuses this idea by looking closely at the typical interactive routines and activities that children in a local community typically engage in throughout their development from birth through high school graduation to ensure that their needs and desires are met. This comprehensive approach fully embraces the holistic notions that:

1. The activities and interactions children engage in involve the same overlapping agencies, institutions, and others who serve them (e.g., medical services; dental services; nutrition services; community sports, arts, music, museum, and library programs).
2. Schools are in the most ideal position to support and align these various entities so that they work efficiently, effectively, *and* seamlessly.

As such, a culturally responsive partnership approach is grounded in the belief that schools are an integral partner of the community to ensure that the scope of supports and services that are provided to its children are on behalf of their social-emotional, physical, and academic success in order to be active and participating members of our local and global communities. Further, it requires that they address any barriers or obstacles that might interfere with the type of membership and participation needed to support a child's optimal development. That calls for a school-based examination to really understand and look deeply at the different barriers, obstacles, and assets of the students.

Let's look at what might seem like a small example of second-grade students in a mathematics class to see one of the conditions needed for a culturally responsive school. In this example, the majority of second graders in a particular community plays soccer. Their parents/guardians are deeply familiar with the dates, times, and steps needed to enroll their child in their community's soccer program. These include the following:

- making sure that their child has the required physical exam to be cleared to play the sport;
- purchasing the necessary sports equipment, including shin and mouth guards, for their child;
- familiarity with the rules and rituals that govern their child's participation; and

- understanding this after-school and/or weekend activity is an integral, ritualized part of their child's development.

To push our point a bit further, the parents also understand that the soccer activity ensures that their child engages in physical exercise, something they view as essential to their child's well-being. They also believe it is an important activity for building their child's social skills. In addition, soccer (known as fútbol by members of a Latino community) is often an important cultural activity for many. In this sense, this one activity is valued as an integral part of a child's life by many. Let's also look at it from an interactive perspective. Let's say that we have the privilege of observing two second-grade students engaging in a social conversation about their soccer playing experience. Their conversation goes something like:

WILLIE: "We get to play soccer Thursday!"
THOMAS: "I like drills."
WILLIE: "Me too. I like running!"
THOMAS: "Me too! I think we will run one million miles!"
WILLIE: "Two million miles!"

Their back-and-forth banter shows a depth of understanding about the soccer/fútbol activity. We also note that their second-grade teacher knows that boys and girls in this particular second-grade class participate in their community's soccer program and that she wants to create an activity that connects their experience to the mathematics standard the students are studying—namely, to be able to describe and analyze the sides and angles of shapes (Massachusetts Mathematics Curriculum Framework, 2017). Using an activity that she believes all of her students will participate in, the teacher decides that a soccer example to learn about shapes will be a great way to support students' engagement in mathematics. She creates a math activity that involves finding shapes on a soccer field and acknowledges that some students refer to the game as fútbol. Most of her students are successfully able to actively engage in the activity by naming a variety of shapes they observe. However, some of the students are not yet able to engage in the mathematics task because they do not have the experience needed to build these powerful engaging connections.

Figure 6.2 illustrates the steps that the teacher took to connect the mathematics standard to students' life experiences.

One of the classic problems in the task activity that the second-grade teacher created is that it engaged some but not all of a classroom of students. The same holds true for many textbooks, despite their good intentions; namely, an assumption is made that all students have the same prior social-cultural or life experiences needed to engage in the examples and activities included (Zacarian, 2015).

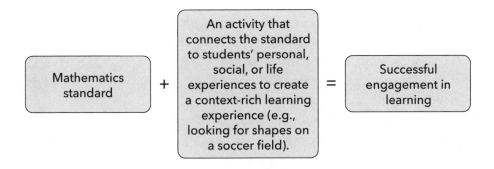

Figure 6.2: Application of a Content Standard to Students' Life Experiences

In our soccer example, a few students were unable to engage in the problem because they did not participate in the community's soccer program and/or had no prior knowledge of the sport. As such, the mathematics problem does not have the depth of connections coupled with the life experiences that are needed for the students to learn and even master the mathematics content. If we step back and consider this example, we could easily substitute another one which would help us to see that we often make assumptions about our students' lives. Let's substitute the soccer example with a new one. Let's say that the same second grade teacher makes the assumption that all second graders eat pizza and that a great activity would be to identify different shapes using the pizza example. Just as our soccer example led to a few students being unable to engage in the problem, the same may be true of the pizza example. We must be sure to check that the examples that we use to draw on students' life experiences are based on their actual life experiences and not our assumptions about them.

A Comprehensive Exploration of Obstacles, Barriers, and Assets

In Chapter 1, we discussed two seminal theoretical underpinnings of culturally relevant pedagogy (Ladson-Billings, 1995). First, that it involves looking closely at conceptions of ourselves and others and, second, that we expand our work with students beyond their academic well-being to a more holistic focus (Ladson-Billings, 1995). These two underpinnings are essential for working with local community partners. Let's go back to the assumption that all second-grade students play soccer or go to the dentist. Both, according to developmental and community psychologist scholar Hirokazu Yoshikawa, involve a family's social ties, resources, and benefits on behalf of their child's development (Yoshikawa, 2011). This is an important concept to consider. As educators, we can easily make assumptions about our students in a myriad of ways because we are not familiar enough with their social ties, resources, and benefits. One reason for this lack of information was presented in our first chapter; namely, that most educators are White or White and middle class and teach students who are increasingly culturally, linguistically, economically, and racially diverse (Edwards et al., 2017). Further, we also shared that half of the nation's students live in poverty and more than half have had one or more significantly adverse childhood experience.

Making assumptions about those we educate, despite our good intentions, commitment, and dedication to the profession, can easily occur when we perceive that all students have similar experiences. That stance can greatly hamper our capacity to create a holistic approach because we might easily assume that our students wouldn't benefit from, or even worse, don't need community partner resources and benefits when, in reality, they are very much needed and we should be tapping into these wholeheartedly.

For example, Yoshikawa studied the influence of undocumented family status on a child's development. He found that these families had far fewer social ties to a community, resources, and benefits to improve their child's development and that their children were far less likely to experience many of the same services and supports as their peers, including early education and care (Yoshikawa, 2011). Further, he also found that the lack of capacity to use these resources can and does have a powerful effect on children. Many scholars have found similar outcomes for students living in poverty, English learners, students of color, and other groups of culturally and linguistically diverse students whose families lack the understanding, resources, and benefits needed for a child's success (Duncan-Andrade, 2009; Goldenberg & Coleman, 2012; Gay, 2010; Gamoran & Long, 2006; Ladson-Billings, 1994, 1995). In Chapter 1, we also explored key historic Supreme Court cases and federal laws that were passed to address the pervasive inequalities and discriminatory practices that occurred nation-wide and improve the outcomes of culturally diverse students (see Chapter 1, Figure 1.1: Historic Timeline of Key Court Cases and Federal Regulations and Initiatives). We also stated that while these actions should have resulted in compliance, disparities have prevailed among and between different groups of students (see Figure 1.2: U.S. Public School Graduation Rates, 2015–2016).

1. Describe two to three disparities you have observed in a school setting.

_____

_____

_____

2. What do you believe are the key reasons for these disparities?

_____

_____

_____

3. What has been done to address these in ways that have been successful or not successful?

_____

_____

_____

CREATING AN ASSET-BASED, SCHOOL-BASED TEAM

It is much more possible to address the needs and desires of culturally and linguistically diverse students when we work collaboratively. Many might do this by using a deficit-based approach about what they perceive is missing in the lives of students. We pose that it must instead be based on addressing the needs and affirming the strengths of students to reach their optimal potential. It calls for looking carefully at how we can work closely with students, families, and the community. A first step for doing this is to create a school-based team that represents members who:

- can offer representation and/or understanding of the cultural and linguistic diversity of its diverse student and family populations;
- affirm the strengths and assets of diverse students and families;
- continuously look at ways in which culturally and linguistically diverse students can be empowered, contributing, and participatory members of their classroom and school communities; and
- select a school–community liaison or liaisons that will assist in recruiting; in building positive, asset-based, school–community partnerships; and in supporting these to be sustained and enduring; plus have the capacity to change over time to continuously meet the changing needs and assets of students and their families.

EXAMINING THE VARIOUS "LOCAL" SECTORS OF CHILD'S DEVELOPMENT

Two of the most important and continuous tasks of a school-based team is to be intentional in examining the various sectors necessary for a child's holistic development and seek real solutions to any barriers or obstacles that occur. Figure 6.3 is intended to provide us with a map for engaging in such an examination. A first and important task reflects what we described in Chapter 5: to examine our own biases and assumptions about what we believe we understand. Our soccer example is one. In it, we see that the teacher created a task she thought would relate to all of the students in her class because she assumed that all students play the game and that their

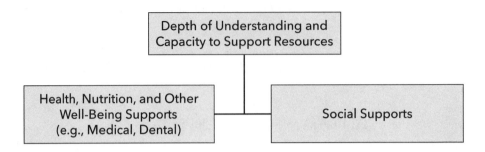

Figure 6.3: Educators' Knowledge of Family's Social Ties, Resources, and Benefits

common experience would successfully engage all of them in finding mathematics shapes. The second example that we furnish is that all students go to the dentist. The upper most box of Figure 6.3 asks a two-part question:

- What understanding is needed for a child to engage in a health, nutrition, and well-being activity as well as a social activity that commonly occurs in the local community?
- Do all families have the capacity to support the resources needed for this activity or these activities?

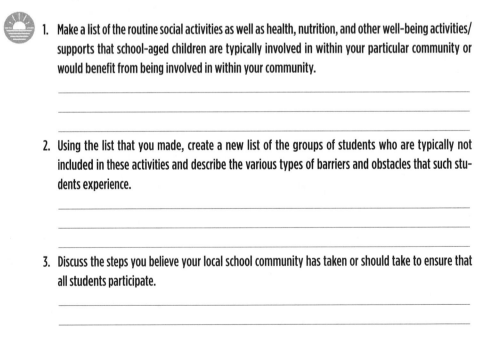

1. Make a list of the routine social activities as well as health, nutrition, and other well-being activities/supports that school-aged children are typically involved in within your particular community or would benefit from being involved in within your community.

    _____

    _____

    _____

2. Using the list that you made, create a new list of the groups of students who are typically not included in these activities and describe the various types of barriers and obstacles that such students experience.

    _____

    _____

    _____

3. Discuss the steps you believe your local school community has taken or should take to ensure that all students participate.

    _____

    _____

    _____

In general terms, families engage their children in a variety of sectors during their development. Some of these might seem obvious, including the medical and dental supports all children should have, and some might seem less obvious, such as the community soccer program we included in our earlier example. Each of these sectors form a holistic and important way of thinking about a child's development. If we look back to Yoshikawa's contributions, we find that his research showed that some children, particularly citizen children of undocumented families and undocumented children, are far less likely to receive the much-needed support of medical, dental, and overall health care, let alone be involved in a community soccer program (Yoshikawa, 2011). The same holds true for many children in need of medical, dental, and nutritional supports, such as those who often go without, including children who are homeless, living in deep poverty, and others. Examining these sectors of a child's development (medical, dental, nutritional, and housing) helps to ensure that a child's basic needs are met. While some educators might argue that schools should not be engaging in this work—even though there is no doubt these supports are major necessities in students' lives—organizations such as the Association of Supervision and Curriculum Development have declared that these supports and others are critical for a whole community, whole school, whole child approach (2019b). Among the various sectors they include are the following, shown in the following list:

Figure 6.4: Various Sectors of Support

- Physical education and physical activity
- Nutritional environment and services
- Health services
- Counseling, psychological, and social services
- Social and emotional climate
- Physical environment
- Family engagement
- Community involvement (ASCD, 2019b).

1. Think about the soccer program we described in an earlier example. Do you believe that it should be provided only to the children whose parents understand the benefits of physical exercise and can afford it or that it should be provided to all children? Why?

_____

_____

_____

2. In addition to the list provided in Figure 6.4, what are some other supports/services you believe are critical to add to those offered in your local context and why?

_____

_____

_____

_____

_____

RESOURCE TOOLS FOR TEAM ANALYSIS OF NEEDS

Drawing from Figure 6.4, conduct an analysis of the various sectors students are involved in, the barriers and obstacles that some students experience, and make recommendations for school–community partnerships. Figures 6.5, 6.6, 6.7, 6.8, 6.9, and 6.10 provide tools for analyzing physical, social, nutritional, health, counseling/psychological, and additional activities.

Figure 6.5: Physical Education and Activities

Type of Analysis	Findings and Recommendations
1. Physical exercise activities children are typically involved with in our particular community	
2. Activities children would benefit from being involved with in our community	
3. Students who are typically not included in these activities and types of barriers and obstacles that prevent involvement	
4. Potential partners that might support solutions to barriers and obstacles	
5. Potential partners that might support solutions to student participation in medical health, dental health, nutrition, and other well-being activities	

Figure 6.6: Social Activities

Type of Analysis	Findings and Recommendations
1. Social activities children are typically involved with in our particular community	
2. Activities children would benefit from being involved with in our community	
3. Students who are typically not included in these activities and types of barriers and obstacles that prevent involvement	
4. Potential partners that might support solutions to barriers and obstacles	
5. Potential partners that might support solutions to student participation in medical health, dental health, nutrition, and other well-being activities	

Figure 6.7: Nutritional Services

Type of Analysis	Findings and Recommendations
1. Activities children are typically involved with in our particular community	
2. Activities children would benefit from being involved with in our community	
3. Students who are typically not included in these activities and types of barriers and obstacles that prevent involvement	
4. Potential partners that might support solutions to barriers and obstacles	
5. Potential partners that might support solutions to student participation in medical health, dental health, nutrition, and other well-being activities	

Figure 6.8: Health Services

Type of Analysis	Findings and Recommendations
1. Activities children are typically involved with in our particular community	
2. Activities children would benefit from being involved with in our community	
3. Students who are typically not included in these activities and types of barriers and obstacles that prevent involvement	
4. Potential partners that might support solutions to barriers and obstacles	
5. Potential partners that might support solutions to student participation in medical health, dental health, nutrition, and other well-being activities	

Figure 6.9: Counseling, Psychological, and Social Services

Type of Analysis	Findings and Recommendations
1. Activities children are typically involved with in our particular community	
2. Activities children would benefit from being involved with in our community	
3. Students who are typically not included in these activities and types of barriers and obstacles that prevent involvement	
4. Potential partners that might support solutions to barriers and obstacles	
5. Potential partners that might support solutions to student participation in medical health, dental health, nutrition, and other well-being activities	

Figure 6.10: Additional Services

Type of Analysis	Findings and Recommendations
1. Activities children are typically involved with in our particular community	
2. Activities children would benefit from being involved with in our community	
3. Students who are typically not included in these activities and types of barriers and obstacles that prevent involvement	
4. Potential partners that might support solutions to barriers and obstacles	
5. Potential partners that might support solutions to student participation in medical health, dental health, nutrition, and other well-being activities	

For example, Wolfe Street Academy engaged in this type of analysis to determine the needs of its students and community. That analysis resulted in acquiring an asset-based partner that would be able to communicate with its growing number of Spanish-speaking students and families. According to Dr. Clemencia Vargas, University of Maryland School of Dentistry partner:

> "When we do programs for Latino parents, we are using—they're curriculum-based, so we define very clearly what we want to talk about, and we are very sensitive to being culturally aware, so if we're talking with Latino parents, we will talk, of course, in Spanish. That is the first part.
>
> And usually we have students who are native speakers. We will talk about their own food. We use the music. We use their customs, their beliefs." *(Dr. Clemencia Vargas, University of Maryland School of Dentistry, 2019)*

The type of partnership that Dr. Vargas is referring to is one that is culturally and linguistically responsive and draws on the assets and strengths of students and families. It calls for us all to identify community partners that will support us in acknowledging and valuing students' and families' assets and competencies and to address their needs.

IDENTIFYING LOCAL PARTNERS

It is key for a school-based team to identify and recruit local resources (e.g., individuals, associations, institutions, and organizations) that can work as a partner to address needs and support the assets of its students. Below are steps for collaboratively engaging in this identification and recruitment activity.

1. Select a point person or team that will act as a liaison(s) or the primary communicator(s) with community partners to support a strong school–community relationship and ensure that it is as seamless and efficient as possible.
   - An example of what can happen when this does *not* occur is a middle school student who needs dental care and each of his teachers, unbeknownst to the others, calls their individual dentists to recruit their help.
2. Seek a community partner who will support creating a mutually beneficial partnership.
   - A powerful example is Wolfe Street Academy in Baltimore, Maryland, and the longstanding partnership it has forged with the University of Maryland School of Dentistry.

Wolfe Street Academy and the University of Maryland School of Dentistry

Ten years ago, Wolfe Street's students suffered from many dental challenges (Vargas, 2019). Wolfe Street Academy sought a community partner that would address the challenges its students were experiencing, enhance their strengths, and grow and change with its students. According to Dr. Vargas, the partnership initially began by addressing the significant challenges the students were having, including those from undocumented families who had never had dental care.

Once these were addressed, the focus of the community-school partnership shifted to support the ever-changing needs and desires of Wolfe Street Academy's students and families as well as the aspirations of the University of Maryland's School of Dentistry (Vargas, 2019). For example, once the dental issues were addressed, the partnership shifted its focus to strengthening students' dental hygiene and nutritional practices. When the university received funding from an outside source, it sought out Wolfe Street Academy to expand the partnership to include after-school programming (Vargas, 2019).

Another hallmark of this school–community partnership is to seek ways to partner with families that will also be of benefit to the university's dental students. For example, since parents come to the school for a morning meeting, their dental school partner viewed that time slot as an opportunity to get to know and work with families in support of their children's dental and nutritional health. Additionally, the partnership expanded to spark Wolfe Street Academy students' interests in the dental field. Older students at Wolfe Street Academy engage in dentistry apprenticeships, where they hold the exam light and assist dental professionals during screenings.

The dental partners also work closely with families by honoring and valuing their cultural ways of being. In speaking about the partnership, Dr. Vargas talks about its mutual value. She describes the reciprocal relationships and positive possibilities that have occurred by working with dentistry interns who are familiar with the language, cultural practices, and beliefs of Wolfe Street's families and who create relationships grounded in empowering families and students as partners. For example, she speaks about the involvement of fifth-grade students in helping make dentistry accessible to their younger peers.

> "At this time, the fifth graders, we have seen them since first grade, so the older children already come here and talk to us, and they are helpers, and they want to, like you saw today, the girl holding the light, she wanted to be part of it.
>
> And so [she] could understand, and she'd talk about molars. So those are wonderful stories and make dentistry—they make dentistry more accessible to the children. And maybe they will think about becoming dentists. You never know."
> *(Vargas, 2019)*

Creating Partnerships that are Mutually Beneficial, Enduring, and Transformative

Emblematic of the type of school–community partnerships we are referring to is that they are mutually beneficial and work to have a positive effect on the individuals and groups involved so that they can and do grow and transform together by continuously focusing on the ever-changing needs of students. Wolfe Street's partnership with the University of Maryland's School of Dentistry is but one example of the type of enduring partnership we are referring to. While it started as a partnership to ensure that the school provided dental screenings for its students, it has evolved over the past decade to include nutritional counseling, working with families, and student-dental intern partnerships. The partnership incorporated the three key elements of a school–community partnership that we presented earlier in this chapter. It (1) took time to identify a need (dental care) that would benefit from a community partner, (2) found a community partner that would address the needs they identified and support the school's assets, and (3) created the long-lasting and transformative partnership they have forged together.

Describe a potential school–community partnership you might forge. How will you be sure it acknowledges and honors the assets and competencies of your focal students and families? What types of activities might you engage in to ensure that it is long-lasting and transformative? _____

_____

_____

_____

_____

_____

_____

EMBRACING PROFESSIONAL DEVELOPMENT PARTNERSHIPS TO SUPPORT RESPONSIVE SCHOOLS

The partnerships we build to create responsive schools for culturally and linguistically diverse students must include educators acquiring the skills and practices that are needed. These include taking stock of what we are currently doing to move away from a deficit- and/or myth-based approach about students and their families toward a strengths-based approach. Doing this requires that schools or districts engage in a collaborative assessment to identify what we don't know and need to learn so that we may strengthen the ways in which we support our students to be successful in school and in their lives. Figure 6.11 provides methods for engaging in an analysis of professional development needs. The first and second questions are intended for individuals to complete. The third and fourth questions are intended for a group to engage in when examining its professional growth needs. The questions for individuals and groups are intended to support a school- or district-based team in identifying its professional growth needs. The fifth and final question is intended for the team to pinpoint potential community-based partners that might provide the professional development that has been identified.

A powerful example of what we are describing is the Brockton Public Schools' partnership with Bridgewater State University's Pedro Pires Institute for Cape Verdean Studies in Massachusetts. Close to 41% of Brockton's public school families' first language is not English and 58% of its English learners are from the West African country of Cabo Verde (also known as Cape Verde). In an effort to strengthen its understanding of its Cape Verdean students and their families, the public school district partnered with the institute at Bridgewater State University. In addition to its mission to foster scholarly research and engagement, the Pedro Pires

Figure 6.11: Team Analysis for Professional Development Partners

Type of Analysis	Findings
1. Self-assessment of professional development topics needed to address the social-emotional and academic needs of the culturally and linguistically diverse students with whom I work.	
2. Steps I would like to take to obtain professional development to address these identified needs.	
3. Group-assessment of professional development topics needed to address the social-emotional and academic needs of the culturally and linguistically diverse students with whom our school district works.	
4. Steps we will take to obtain professional development to address these identified needs.	
5. Potential partners that might support our professional development activities.	

Institute "fosters knowledge production and dissemination, while highlighting the culture of Cape Verde" (Pedro Pires Institute for Cape Verdean Studies, n.d.). One of the hopes and dreams of one of the district-based partners, Kellie Jones, director of its English learners program, was to have educators from the public school community, under the direction of the Pedro Pires Institute, travel to Cape Verde to experience the country and culture firsthand (Jones, July 25, 2019, personal communication). With agreement and some financial support from the district and school committee, nine public school staff and administrators traveled to Cape Verde during the spring 2019 break with Professor David Almeida from the institute to learn about the cultural and linguistic backgrounds of its Cape Verdean students. According to Jones,

" . . . I always talk about wanting teachers to understand the background and experiences of the students, but not limit students based on that understanding. I want educators to see the kids' assets that they bring to the district. And I believe that the participants definitely walked away from the experience with seeing students' strengths. And it's a powerful statement to students. You are important to me. You are so important to me that I want to know everything about you. You are so important to me that I will use my vacation and own money to go and learn about your country, culture, and language. Wow—that's powerful for students to know how important they are to faculty." *(Jones, July 25, 2019)*

An ESL teacher who participated in the trip reflected that, "By seeing our potential students engaged in learning in their native language and in their home school, I now have a new way of looking at our new arrivals. They are like a well-packed suitcase. We have to carefully and patiently unfold all of their 'belongings' before we find the buried treasure: The whole child." (Jones, July 25, 2019).

The experience was so successful that it is slated to occur again, professional connections have been made between the ministry of education and the U.S. consulate in Cabo Verde, and conversations are underway to explore the possibilities of traveling to the home countries of other groups of students.

In our next chapter, we will focus on the key principles and approaches for students to contribute to their school and local communities through service-learning projects in which they address issues relevant to the school/district communities in which they learn and local and global communities in which they live.

7

Service-learning as a Culturally Responsive Practice

AT WHITTIER COLLEGE, Professors Ivannia Soto and Natale Zappia teamed up to create service-learning assignments for students enrolled in their courses, "Issues in Urban Education" and "Early American Environmental History." One of their important goals was to bring the coursework alive by engaging students in firsthand experiences. Here is what one student wrote as part of a reflection essay about the experience.

> . . . we spent a lot of time working with ELL students and so it was really cool to get a hands-on experience with them and I think it kind of cemented that portion of the course really well for me. Also, what I really remember and took away from it was the achievement gap. And what I actually learned beyond the classroom, it's not just an academic achievement gap between like the wealthy and the poor or whites and minorities. *(personal communication with Nick Stanton, January 2015)*

This chapter will focus on the key principles and approaches for public school students and pre- and in-service educators to contribute to their school and local communities through service-learning projects in which they address issues that are relevant to the school/district communities in which they learn and local communities in which they live. We have specifically included pre- and in-service educators to support the important practice of engagement in authentic experiences to learn from and benefit the community in a meaningful way. In this chapter we will:

- define service-learning, including a brief overview of seminal researchers who developed the theoretical framework for the field;
- discuss service-learning as a national equity issue as it is far more prevalent in K–12 schools located in geographic areas with middle- and high-income populations as opposed to it being equally available in geographic areas with low-income populations—as a result, some students experience a range of service-learning experiences while others do not;
- unpack qualities of service-learning as they apply to K–12 as well as college students, describe service-learning models, and provide key steps for developing K–12 and college service-learning units;
- describe the steps needed for creating meaningful and engaging culturally responsive service-learning projects within a school/district as a means to cement and infuse the principles presented in our book; and
- detail the importance of securing and partnering with culturally responsive businesses and community-based agency partners.

WHAT IS SERVICE-LEARNING?

According to the Center for Service-Learning and Civic Engagement Toolkit (2015) developed by Michigan State University, service-learning is, "A teaching method that combines academic coursework with the application of institutional resources (e.g., knowledge and expertise of students, faculty and staff, political position, buildings and land) to address challenges facing communities through collaboration with these communities. This pedagogy focuses on critical, reflective thinking to develop students' academic skills, sense of civic responsibility, and commitment to the community." As such, the essence of service-learning is a culturally responsive practice, especially when commitment to the community and a sense of civic responsibility are intentionally well developed by educators.

Four pivotal contributors to the field of service-learning include John Dewey (1910, 1933, 1938), David Kolb (1984), Paulo Freire (1994, 1998, 2001), and Gloria Ladson-Billings (1995). The four promote the idea that transformative education occurs when students are actively involved in their own learning and experience mutual exchange with their communities. Dewey, who focused on cycles of action and reflection, initially proposed experiential learning theories. Kolb then added to Dewey's work by exploring observation, reflection, and analysis in empowering students to become responsible for and engaged in their own learning. Freire, known for his work on critical pedagogy, advanced the field by breaking down the traditional power dynamic between teacher and student. He emphasized the importance of students being actively involved and invested in their own learning, and students and teachers co-creating and exchanging knowledge. Freire also suggested that service approaches should "empower" communities and treat community members with dignity and respect. In addition, Ladson-Billings advanced these ideas by helping us to see the links that can be made between engaging students meaningfully with the community and social change (Ladson-Billings, 1995, pp. 156–157). Indeed, she defines culturally responsive teaching as "a pedagogy that empowers students intellectually, socially, emotionally, and politically . . ." (p. 20). Expanding this a bit further, Bassey (2016) defines service-learning as an opportunity for students to "develop a commitment to service as well as social justice ideals (p. 5)." She helps us to see that service-learning is not a means to an end. Rather, its goal is to help raise students' awareness of social injustices and engage them in meaningful actions that support change (p. 3). As such, service-learning projects or units should be intentionally and carefully designed with these theoretical constructs in mind, whether in K–12 or higher education settings.

WHY IS SERVICE-LEARNING AN EQUITY ISSUE IN K–12 SETTINGS?

In 2008, the Education Commission of the States published a research-based advocacy paper about the importance of service-learning in K–12 settings. Synthesizing 20 years of research on the learning approach, the report begins with a description about the many strengths of using this approach:

> "A growing body of research describes the positive impact service-learning can have on young people. Well-implemented service-learning can help them achieve academically; strengthen their job and career-related skills and aspirations; and increase their self-efficacy, respect for diversity, self-confidence, collaborative skills, avoidance of risk behaviors, and resilience. A significant part of the research examines the potential of service-learning to help young people develop civic skills, attitudes and behaviors." *(Pickeral, Lennon, & Piscatelli, 2008, p. 1)*

With all of these positives for service-learning, unfortunately, it is not an approach that is practiced across the nation and it should be. It was enacted broadly when President George H. W. Bush signed the National Community Service Act in

1990 and President Clinton signed the National Community and Service Trust Act in 1993, allowing schools to apply for federal grant funding to support the approach. However, within two decades, many schools began dropping service-learning from their practices. The year 2011 marked a deep decline in the number of schools and districts that engaged students in service-learning, particularly in low-income districts where high-stakes test readiness was a top priority and service-learning was, unfortunately, seen as a luxury (Ryan, 2012). As we will discuss further in this chapter, service-learning is a critical approach for making learning more meaningful and students more empowered as citizens of their local and global communities. While some states award students credits toward graduation for their service-learning experiences, precious few encourage it as a practice of a students' education (Education Commission, January 2014).

Responsive schooling for culturally and linguistically diverse students requires that we reconsider the tremendous benefits of its application, particularly as it applies to the very students that have been sorely affected by its absence—those in low-income communities. To do that requires that we rethink how it can be operationalized in K–12 settings across the socio-economic spectrum *and* look carefully at how we can systematically include it in all teacher education programs to better ensure that our teaching and educational leadership force engages in its practice as part of a responsive school practice.

1. Do service-learning initiatives occur in the local community in which you work or live?

   _____

   _____

   _____

2. If you responded yes to question 1, describe one initiative and its goals.

   _____

   _____

   _____

3. Did you engage in service-learning as part of your school and/or college experience? If yes, describe the experience. If not, how might it have advanced your understanding of serving the community to respond to a need?

   _____

   _____

   _____

FEATURES OF K–12 SERVICE-LEARNING

The Education Commission (2014) highlights some of the key features that support service-learning to be fully operational and sustained over time. The following explains these features and includes some examples of them. These key features are considered best practices and guidelines for developing K–12 service-learning projects.

- First and foremost, it must be supported by all "education stakeholders, including teachers, school leaders, district administrators and state policymakers" (Pickeral, Lennon, & Piscatelli, 2008, p. 1). While this is key to its success, one of the most challenging aspects in doing this, they tell us, is helping everyone to see and fully embrace the research evidence that shows the many positive effects and long-lasting effects that service-learning has on students' academic achievement, responsibility, and citizenry. As we will discuss in our next section, while it should be an essential component to every student's education, precious few provide service-learning experiences to its students. It calls for us to rethink the many advantages of engaging students in activities that benefit their learning and community.

- A service-learning project must also address a real need or desire in the community. It is not enough to simply engage students with community members; it must be for a real purpose. An example that we will detail later in this chapter is a group of elementary school students who are at the beginning stages of learning English and aren't yet able to comprehend subject matter content delivered in English. To remedy this challenge, high school students who are enrolled in a dual language program provide much-needed tutorial supports in the students' homes languages. This service-learning activity addresses a real need in the district.

- Additionally, students must engage in planning and preparing for a service-learning project in a meaningful and purposeful way. While choosing a service-learning focus is essential (e.g., supporting young beginning learners of English), there are a number of critical steps and decisions that must be made by students and their teachers to actually engage in the service-learning project successfully. These include selecting the learning goals that will be achieved as a result of the experience, as well as the background information and practical training that students need to engage in the service-learning experience successfully. For example, as we will describe later in the chapter, the high school tutors needed to prepare and plan to engage their young learners in a meaningful learning experience over a sustained period of time.

- The service-learning project must also include a hands-on authentic experience. This allows students to readily apply what they are learning in a real-life setting. An example is the high school tutors who worked with young learners to support their understanding of subject matter.
- Allow students to take responsibility and exercise their own agency and empowerment to engage in the service-learning experience. An important feature of service-learning is its dependence on being flexible for whatever can occur as it is occurring. Our tutorial example is a fine one for explaining the need for flexibility. Let's say that a high school or college student has prepared to tutor a young student in math. Working with his high school teacher, he takes time to craft a lesson they think will be of keen interest to the student and match what the student is learning that week. On the day of the tutorial, the tutor learns that his tutee is absent from school and will be out the rest of the week. Empowered with this information, he meets with his high school teacher and crafts a new lesson for the student to engage in when he returns.
- It is also critical that any partnership be established and sustained over time and that it has the capacity and flexibility to change as the needs and desires of the community and students change. An example of the type of flexibility we are describing is service-learning projects targeted to support their community. In this chapter, we include an example of a high school medical interpretation certification program that is targeted to serve its local Spanish-, Cape Verdean Creole–, and Haitian Creole–speaking community.
- Engage students in actively thinking about, reflecting on, and rethinking what they are learning and applying it in a way that is meaningful and purposeful. As we will explain in the next segment of this chapter, supporting continuous reflection is a hallmark of any service-learning project and is the fourth of five stages or steps of the *K–12 Service-Learning Toolkit* (RMC Research Corporation [2009]).

1. Think of a service-learning initiative you have engaged or engaged others in.

_____

_____

_____

_____

2. Describe the ways that its features support it to be fully operational and sustained over time.

_____

_____

_____

_____

The RMC Research Corporation (2009) published a *K-12 Service-Learning Toolkit* for Learn and Serve America's National Service-Learning Clearinghouse. It includes five stages or steps for engaging students in a service-learning project. In the following section, we look at each stage and include two authentic service-learning examples: the Brockton Public Schools in Brockton, Massachusetts, and the Framingham Public Schools, in Framingham, Massachusetts. Both districts have high incidences of students who are fluent in two languages. Brockton provides a variety of language programming including dual immersion programs in Spanish, Portuguese, and French; transitional bilingual education programs; and structured English immersion programming. In addition, Brockton's classical and modern language learning offers a broad range of programming. According to its coordinator Rachael Umbrianno, "Sixth-grade students who are not already in an immersion program get a chance to choose Mandarin, Latin, or Spanish, depending on the offerings at their middle schools and students can also jump in at grade nine" (personal communication, August 21, 2019). In addition, Brockton's classical and modern language programming includes a medical interpretation certification program in Spanish, French/Haitian, and Portuguese/Cape Verdean that commences during students' junior year in high school. Students are given a language assessment to demonstrate they are at least highly proficient to be accepted into this course of study. Framingham has a highly diverse student population serving students from more than 70 different countries and offers a range of programming for its English learners and fluent English speakers, including two-way Spanish bilingual, two-way Portuguese bilingual, transitional bilingual education for its Portuguese- and Spanish-speaking English learners, sheltered English immersion programming, and a Seal of Biliteracy for students completing its two-way programming. Drawing from the students' linguistic assets, the two districts created service-learning programs to address a community need. Let's look at the five stages and examples from the two districts.

1. **Investigation:** The first phase of a service-learning project involves engaging students in exploring a community need they might address as they engage in an academic learning experience. This initial phase should include a range of activities to spark students' interest in addressing the problem and develop consensus in the ways that it will be addressed. These might include a classroom brainstorming discussion (e.g., where students engage in pairs, small groups, and/or as a whole class); engaging in research about the problem and solutions that have occurred (such as reading newspaper accounts); and collaboratively developing an observation protocol for students to see the need firsthand. These might also occur as part of a specific course of study that is

designed to provide a structured, systematized program of service-learning study as well as a less formal program. Both can be highly successful. Let's look at a highly successful, formal service-learning experience in the Brockton Public Schools and a second highly successful yet less formal service-learning experience at the Framingham Public Schools.

- Example 1: Rachael Umbrianna, coordinator of classical and modern languages, Brockton Public Schools, Brockton, Massachusetts (personal communication, August 21, 2019).

   "The former coordinator of Brockton's classical and modern languages convened a committee over 15 years ago to learn about successful medical interpretation programs in schools across America and explore the possibilities of a course of study that would apply to high school students. Our goal was to create a program that would support high school students to provide a service that is needed in our community and support them in the effort. The medical interpretation program is available in Spanish, Haitian Creole and Cape Verdean Creole; as these are the most common languages spoken in addition to English in our city."

- Example 2: Genoveffa Greici, director, bilingual programming, Framingham Public Schools, Framingham, Massachusetts (personal communication, November 14, 2019).

   "Framingham Public Schools is well known in the MetroWest area (west of Boston) for its varied offerings of bilingual programs, including Dual Language, Transitional Bilingual, Heritage Language, World Language and Sheltered Immersion programs, to support instruction for emerging multilingual learners. The Dual Language Spanish program, from preschool to grade 12, has been in existence in the Framingham Public School System for 25 years. Students who have participated in the Spanish DL program since kindergarten and are now seniors in high school are eligible for the State SEAL of Biliteracy, internship opportunities for using Spanish in the community, and possibilities for dual enrollment at local universities in Spanish Language and Culture. At FPS we strongly support socio-cultural competence, one of the pillars of DL education. Tenets of our mission statement is celebrating students' cultural, linguistic and educational backgrounds, practices, and experiences.

   As seniors, students in the DL programs participate in internship opportunities in their school and community as a way of giving back, using their linguistic resources and find ways of connecting and building relationships with people. There are many options for students to partic-

ipate in: volunteering at the elementary and middle schools DL classes as language tutors, interpreting at hospitals and other local community organizations to support bilingual families who are not proficient in English, and oftentimes also working in local Spanish businesses in our city. In all of these situations graduating students are able to demonstrate their fluency in Spanish and to celebrate it using language in a meaningful way. Students love to return to their elementary and middle schools, supporting recent arrivals to the country and school system, supporting teachers in the classroom with newcomers and overall being a great role-model for the new arrivals, or for students who are enrolled in the DL program and learning content in Spanish. For students interested in volunteering at the high school, many of them choose to be teaching assistants in bilingual, ESL, world language classes where they can use their bi and often multilingual skills, others choose to tutor in the ADC (Academic Development Center), the high school tutoring center, and use their bi/multilingual skills as interactive supports for students not yet proficient in English or students learning in Spanish, etc. Students, during a prep time, volunteer in the guidance office and take newcomer students and their families on a tour of the high school. This also helps out guidance counselors who might not speak the family and student's home/native language. All of these volunteering hours count towards the SEAL of Biliteracy district requirements and for younger students, these are the hours which count towards National Honor Society induction and/or used in their college application process. Students keep a log of all of their hours and work with an academic advisor, mostly interested teachers, who support and mentor this work. As students graduate and enroll in college, they continue this volunteering spirit and helping in local organization and college groups."

2. **Planning and preparation:** The second stage involves collaboratively engaging students in determining a specific service-learning project, its goals, and the knowledge and practical information that students need to engage in it. For example, some activities students might engage in include observing or interviewing others, using particular tools or instruments, and meeting with people who have expertise in areas with which the student might not be familiar. As such, students must be supported in the preparation of these projects by helping them to determine and acquire (1) the background information they need about the service-learning recipients and (2) the training they need in how to engage in these activities confidently to address the community need.

- Example 1: Rachael Umbrianna (August 21, 2019)

    "The Committee conducted site visits and investigated the curricula that we would use. They planned the course, developed the structure and created entrance requirements for students, built connections with community organizations to supervise our interns, addressed all legal requirements for external internships with full approval from the school and school committee, and did all this with full support of our district within two years!

    Our students take a course of study during their junior and senior years and then engage in an internship that is 10 hours long and begins in March at area hospitals and health centers. The internship actually occurs after school and on the weekend. Because it is so popular, we want to be sure that everyone has the experience. It is a ten-hour internship. What is great is that several students who complete it provide additional service hours on their own. Seven of the graduates have been employed by a local hospital directly after they obtained their high school diploma!"

    Figure 7.1 provides a description of the course of study that Brockton High School students take to complete the medical interpretation certification program. According to the Brockton High School Guidance Newsletter (2007), students can enroll in the program in their junior year if they have successfully passed the state assessment exams in English language arts and mathematics, have maintained a B or better average in school, are "fully bilingual in Haitian Creole, Cape Verdean Creole, Portuguese, or Spanish and are recommended by their bilingual and English teachers, and [have been] interviewed by the Heads of the Bilingual and Foreign Language Departments [for this program]."

- Example 2: Genoveffa Greici (November 14, 2019)

    "One of the departments most utilized at Framingham High School is the Academic Development Center (ADC), a program targeted to supporting students achieve in their content classes. The uniqueness of this program is that it is student centered, with students tutoring other students. The ADC coordinator pairs students who need help with students who can provide the support. This peer to peer tutoring empowers students to share what they know with students who are not yet comfortable with their new language and content knowledge in a very non-threatening environment. As more students come into the district with educational gaps, limited formal education (SLIFE), or need some short term support in helping them acclimate to their new school, having a cadre of bi-multilingual students to help their peers, in a language they can under-

Figure 7.1: Medical Interpretation Course of Study

Medical Intepretation

MD320	French/Haitian Medical Interpretation I	11	Semester	3
MD321	Portuguese/Cape Verdean Medical Interpretation I	11	Semester	3
MD322	Spanish Medical Interpretation I	11	Semester	3
MD323	French/Haitian Medical Interpretation II	12	Full Year	6
MD324	Portuguese/Cape Verdean Medical Interpretation II	12	Full Year	6
MD325	Spanish Medical Interpretation II	12	Full Year	6
MD326	10-Hour Medical Interpretation Internship	12		1.5

Medical Interpretation and Translation I

French/Haitian Creole MD320, Portuguese/Cape Verdean Creole MD321, Spanish MD322: The goal of this course is to prepare bilingual high school students for interpreting in the workforce. Students will develop an understanding of interpreting standards of practice, concepts and protocols, consistently improve interpreting skills, and learn to self-assess linguistic and cultural knowledge and limitations. Units of study include ethics, local and national laws governing interpreting practice, the culture of medicine, the ethnic cultures of the populations being served, and the culture of being a professional interpreter. These topics will be studied through readings, videos, class discussions and simulated interpreting practice. **NOTE:** Students will being the study of Medical Interpretation and Translation semes... two of the junior year and will continue for a full year of senior year. Application for Coordinator Approval. *****Internship participation is mandatory for this course.**

Medical Interpretation and Translation II

French/Haitian Creole MD323, Portuguese/Cape Verdean Creole MD324, Spanish MD325: This course is a continuation of Medical Interpretation and Translation I. Students will continue to develop an understanding of interpreting standards of practice, concepts and protocols, consistently improve interpreting skills, and learn to self-assess linguistic and cultural knowledge and limitations. **Prerequisite:** Medical Interpretation and Translation I with teacher recommendation and Coordinator Approval. *****Internship participation is mandatory for this course.**

Medical Interpretation Internship MD326: Placement at a local medical facility is available for a ten-hour job shadow/internship for one-half credit to be completed in conjunction with Medical Interpretation II.

(Brockton High School Course of Study, 2019–2020)

stand supports core values, mission and philosophy of the district. The ADC coordinator collaborates with guidance counselors and DHs to identify students who are best matched for this program and who have time in their daily schedules to support it. Students may use this for their service-learning credits which also counts towards graduation require-ments for both tutor and tutee."

3. **Implementation:** The next stage involves launching the service-learning expe-rience. While we might think that teachers take a passive role during this time, a key feature of this stage is the active role that teachers have to pos-itively support students to engage in the service-learning activity and build strong connections between the hands-on experience and what they are learn-ing in class.

   • Example 1: Rachael Umbrianna (August 21, 2019)

     "During the second semester of their junior year, students engage in Medical Interpretation I in one of the three respective languages (Spanish, Haitian Creole, or Cape Verdean Creole). The focus of the course is on the actual 'art' of interpreting and 'bedside manner' of actual situations that might be sensitive or uncomfortable for students. For example, they might role play a scenario where a doctor tells a patient that they are dying, and the students engage in translating this powerful information. They also learn how to and translate medical documents.

     Their senior year includes a full-year course in Medical Interpretation II. The focus of that course is on learning anatomy and physiology and human systems and specific terminology that they will need to engage in this role. During the spring semester, which begins in March, they begin the internship. They do this after school and/or on the weekend and the course provides them with many opportunities to reflect on their intern experience. I work closely with the head of interpretation at the Brockton Neighborhood Health Center around matching our interpretation interns with available interpreters. Our students shadow the interpreters through-out the internship to experience the work."

   • Example 2: Genoveffa Greici (November 14, 2019)

     "The ADC coordinator supports and trains peer tutors to ensure con-sistent processes and protocols are in place such as being on time, com-mitted and responsible for this opportunity. Students who are selected or volunteer at the ADC are generally very invested in the process and want to share and support their peers."

4. **Reflection:** It is essential for students to build connections between what they are experiencing in the service-learning project and what they are learning in class. Engaging students in continuous reflection allows them to understand their own learning and be empowered to learn and be able to identify the skills they are learning and exploring. There are many forms for this key activity, including engaging students in journal writing; writing essays; partner, small-group, and whole-class discussions; responding to writing prompts; providing presentations to specific audiences, and a culminating paper or presentation on the service-learning experience.

   - Example 1: Rachael Umbrianna (August 21, 2019)

     "Reflection is part of the experience of the certification program. We engage students in role-play activities throughout the coursework and in actively reflecting on their internship experience as it is occurring. Students can also apply for a college scholarship if they wish to pursue any type of health-related field. Many apply! Part of that application process is writing an essay about the experience of becoming a medical interpreter. It really helps them to reflect on the experience and us to learn about it as well."

   - Example 2: Genoveffa Greici (November 14, 2019)

     "The ADC coordinator is responsible for overseeing this student program and to constantly communicate with the tutors and tutees who participate. The coordinator also communicates with students' teachers and supervises the students and content instructional activities they participate in. This is an individualized program for students that meets them where they are, being comfortable in learning in a language they are familiar with, English, Spanish and/or Portuguese, the languages of the district."

5. **Demonstration/celebration:** The final stage of a service-learning project involves engaging students in celebrating their accomplishments, acknowledging their efforts, and supporting them in seeing the learning that has occurred. It can also include a celebration that includes community partners that publicly recognizes everyone's efforts to address a need and partner together. Lastly and as importantly, it provides a time for celebrating students' commitment and dedication to their service to others.

   - Example 1: Rachael Umbrianna (August 21, 2019)

     "We have a medical certification ceremony where we invite parents, community partners, alumni from our certification program, our superintendent, and other school officials, as well as juniors who are enrolled

in the first semester of our program. The director of the Brockton Neighborhood Health Center interpretation services speaks at the ceremony and she brings another interpreter to be our keynote speaker. We really believe in our students and the work they are doing. Our celebratory efforts have been acknowledged by the local newspaper."

[An example of the newspaper acknowledgement is seen in Enterprise News, (May 2, 2014).]

- Example 2: Genoveffa Greici (November 14, 2019)

  "Celebrating our students' achievements is key to their successes. As the DL students graduate from a thirteen year educational program in the FPS, the end of the year celebration includes seniors receiving awards for successfully completing the program. Students also receive red and yellow cords they wear at graduation, certificate for having completed the program and acknowledgement of either the STATE Seal of Biliteracy or the STATE SEAL of Biliteracy with Distinction, depending on their assessment data in both English and their partner languages. This end of the year celebration in mid-May is a public acknowledgement of their wonderful accomplishments and includes students, teachers, family and community members. We are always seeking ways to make it better each year and as we expand our dual language programming in the district to include Portuguese DL, we are always looking to find consistency in our implementation practices."

In addition to the two examples we provided, describe a current or future project that infuses or will infuse the five stages of service-learning, or create one.

_____

_____

_____

_____

_____

_____

EXTENDING SERVICE-LEARNING IN HIGHER EDUCATION
TO EXPAND THE PRACTICE OF RESPONSIVE SCHOOLS

As we have discussed in this chapter, students find that the service-learning approach helps them to learn in ways that they had not previously imagined or thought possible. More importantly, it helps all students to be empowered as active participatory citizens who can and do make contributions that make a difference in people's lives. It also greatly helps students to see and examine, firsthand, the complexities of issues they are exploring that they might not otherwise understand fully. This is true for K-12 as well as adult learners, particularly pre- and in-service educators who might not yet have the depth of experience needed to enter our increasingly diverse schools. An example of the type of service-learning that we are referring to is the Presidential Higher Education Community Service Model at Whittier College. Let's take a detailed look at it.

A Presidential Higher Education Community Service Model: "Learning in the Garden"

After completing a service-learning project called "Learning in the Garden," Nick Stanton, a student at Whittier College, reflected on his experience with the following statement on a student gap he noticed besides the learning gap:

> "There's also this other gap, there's this health gap almost. I learned through my research within my group, L.A. is just a very environmentally racist region. And, so you have a lot of students who are exposed to all of these toxins, just because they're poor and that is where they have to live. They come to all these schools and the schools have to deal with that. So that was kind of a major thing that . . . was brand new to me." *(personal communication, January, 2015)*

This quote embodies the transformative power of service-learning projects. Whittier College students like Nick spent a semester observing, reflecting, and analyzing with ELLs at a local high school, and in turn, were empowered to become responsible for and engaged in their own learning, while also giving back to their own communities.

In 2012, for the second year in a row, Whittier College was admitted to President Obama's Higher Education Community Service Honor Roll with distinction for its exemplary commitment to service, developing campus-community partnerships that produce measurable impact engaging students in meaningful service-learning activities. Awarded by the Corporation for National and Community Service (CNCS), the honor with distinction was given to only 110 colleges and universities across the nation. The Corporation for National and Community Service (CNCS) is a federal agency that engages more than five million Americans in service through its Senior Corps, AmeriCorps, and Learn and Serve America programs, and leads President Barack Obama's national call-to-service initiative, *United We Serve* (NationalService.gov). According to Robert Velasco, acting CEO of CNCS:

> "Through service, these institutions are creating the next generation of leaders by challenging students to tackle tough issues and create positive impacts in the community. We applaud the Honor Roll schools, their faculty, and students for their commitment to make service a priority in and out of the classroom. Together, service and learning increase civic engagement while fostering social innovation among students, empowering them to solve challenges within their communities." *(NationalService.gov)*

One of the projects that was awarded President Obama's Higher Education Community Service Honor Roll with distinction at Whittier College in 2012 was the service-learning project called, "Learning in the Garden: A Pedagogical Community Service for English Language Learning and Ecoliteracy at Whittier College." Professors Ivannia Soto (education) and Natale Zappia (history) organized their paired courses (two courses that share a common theme and students—EDUC 250: "Issues in Urban Education" and HIST 359: "Early American Environmental History") to cultivate knowledge with their students inside and outside the walls of the classroom.

Throughout the semester, 22 Whittier College students built and maintained a garden with high school students at La Serna High School in Whittier, California. Whittier College students worked directly with two groups of students at La Serna: English language learners (ELL) participating in a specially designed academic instruction in English (SDAIE) biology class and Advanced Placement (AP) Environmental Science students. La Serna High School is one of six high schools in the Whittier Union High School District (WUHSD) and is the designated school for ELL students at beginning language proficiency levels in the district.

The goals of the garden project were to provide an alternative classroom for students while enriching their environmental literacy and academic language skills. The rationale was to reflect on the use of garden-based activities as pedagogy to enrich the academic English of ELL students. In addition, the project engaged college students in a service-learning project to further develop their understanding of class content (i.e., issues in urban education, achievement gap between students, environmental studies).

The project consisted of six weekly meetings at La Serna High School. Each Whittier College student was responsible for mentoring one ELL student and one AP Environmental Science student. Whittier College students applied their urban agriculture knowledge and teaching techniques by working with ELL students. They dedicated each meeting to teaching new garden concepts (composting, seasons cycle, planting techniques, root system) and science academic vocabulary to their ELL students. The intent of the garden project was to provide an authentic context for ELLs at the high school level to build background knowledge around environmental literacy and develop academic language skills in science. Separately, Whittier College students also worked with their AP Environmental Science students through online journaling, where they reflected on what they learned and accomplished in the garden. The project concluded with one last meeting at Whittier College, where ELL students were invited to tour the campus and worked in the college's community garden.

The paired course with a service-learning component was unique in that introductory courses on urban education and achievement gaps typically require an exploration into historical and contemporary issues shaping public schools, comparing the experiences and underachievement of Latinos, African Americans, and ELLs in K-12 settings, and local school visits and educational documentaries. Similarly, survey courses on environmental history present comparative themes of land use, food systems, and environmental change over time, allowing students to imagine the role of animals, plants, and energy in shaping human ecologies.

While such courses, no doubt, provide important content, opportunities for more innovative and experiential learning can be quite limited. Community service-learning and garden-based education are two effective pedagogical methods augmenting theoretical and historical content learned in classrooms. In recent decades, for example, research on the scholarship of teaching and learning (SoTL) has shown a clear correlation between content mastery, language acquisition, and environmental literacy through service-learning and garden-based education (Miller & J. Moore, 2009). In parallel ways, higher education has also embraced garden-based education through campus student-run farms (Lyle, 1994; Burns and Miller, 2012). The same findings are resonant with K–8 garden-based curricula and programs across the country (Blair, 2009). As these and other recent works indicate, ample opportunities for reciprocal learning can occur across disciplines, curricula, and age groups in service-learning and garden-based classroom settings. Inspired by this growing literature, our project aimed to link high school and college students in a similar SoTL project.

1. **What kinds of community partnerships have you or has your school engaged in? What kinds of community partnerships would you like to engage in?**

_____

_____

_____

_____

2. What kinds of service-learning projects do you see yourself incorporating in your classroom?

_____

_____

_____

WHAT ARE THE QUALITIES OF SERVICE-LEARNING FOR ADULT LEARNERS?

One way to intentionally and carefully design service-learning projects with the above theoretical framework in mind includes being mindful of the six qualities of service-learning developed by the University of Washington Center for Teaching and Learning (2012). These six qualities of service-learning can guide teachers when developing service-learning projects or units and are included below, along with examples of how the Whittier College "Learning in the Garden" service-learning project embodied these six qualities. The six qualities of service-learning include:

1. integrative
2. reflective
3. contextualized
4. strength-based
5. reciprocal
6. lifelong

1. **Integrative:** The service-learning experience goes beyond traditional ideas of classroom learning, practicum training, or off-campus volunteering. Service-learning holistically integrates class learning objectives, faculty guidance, as well as community perspective and priorities. When engaged in genuine service, students participate as both learners and community members. Students demonstrate success both academically and interpersonally.
   • In the Whittier College "Learning in the Garden" service-learning project, college students learned about and served ELLs in their local community by working alongside them to develop a garden and develop ELLs' academic vocabulary.
2. **Reflective:** "The process of reflection is a core component of service-learning. Service-learning practitioners and researchers alike have concluded that the most effective service-learning experiences are those that provide 'structured opportunities' for learners to critically reflect upon their service experience. Structured opportunities for reflection can enable learners to examine and

form the beliefs, values, opinions, assumptions, judgments and practices related to an action or experience, gain a deeper understanding of them and construct their own meaning and significance for future actions." (Moon, 1999, as cited in Conner & Seifer, 2005).

- Whittier College students kept a weekly blog, which highlighted their interactions with ELLs that week, as well as what they learned and how it was connected to course readings or content.

3. **Contextualized:** Service-learning provides students a unique opportunity to access knowledge and expertise that reside in the context of community. There is opportunity to connect the knowledge of a discipline, as explored in class, to the knowledge in practice, as evidenced in communities. Learning experiences in community settings immerse students in the unpredictable and complex nature of real-world situations. Working alongside community members and experienced professionals, the opportunity to construct learning and responses can be immediate and uncontrived.

- Whittier College students learned how the local school district worked and acquired new pedagogical skills by observing their ELLs' biology teacher.

4. **Strength-based:** Service-learning draws upon existing community strengths and resources and honors community members and organizations as co-educators of students. Communities are never built from the outside in. A strength-based approach focuses on the capacity and expertise that exist in every community, rather than on what is absent. By shifting away from a deficit mentality, students learn partnership strategies to identify and develop each community's unique strengths.

- Since each Whittier College student was paired with one ELL, they were able to get to know and build upon students' strengths and assets while also tailoring their teaching to specific needs.

5. **Reciprocal:** The service-learning relationship offers all parties involved some measure of benefits; it is a two-way street. Students give time, talent, and intellectual capital in order to gain deeper understanding of course material and the nuanced nature of social issues. Course instructors modify their teaching practice to include service-learning and are rewarded with deeper student engagement of course material. Community members and organizations invest time as co-educators and, in turn, accomplish more toward their mission and goals through the work of students.

- All parties involved—college professors, the biology teacher, ELLs, and college students—were committed to working with and learning from each other. They had a common goal of developing a school garden by the end of the semester, so they had to work together to do so.

6. **Lifelong:** Service-learning is learning that sticks. By synthesizing theory and practice, this educational method provides a distinctive, meaningful, and influential life experience. Students build relationships, solve problems, value a sense of community, and gain self-awareness. Service-learning is beyond memorable; it can influence one's career path and enhance civic responsibility. Service-learning extends learning beyond the academic term; it lays the foundation for continual personal growth throughout the student's academic experience and beyond.

   • Many Whittier College students decided to continue their relationship with the local high school by taking a course on mentoring in the high school setting, where they were assigned a high school student to mentor weekly. Others decided they wanted to go into the teaching profession as a result of the service-learning experience.

FIRST-YEAR WRITING COURSE WITH SERVICE-LEARNING

Similarly, in 2017, Soto incorporated service-learning into her first-year writing course at Whittier College. Students spent the semester tutoring ELLs while writing essays about their contextualized experiences with them. Each Whittier College first-year student was paired with an ELL at Whittier High School. They began their experience by working with the ELLs around a process called the Road to Reclassification, which teaches ELLs the process and goal setting required to no longer be labeled an ELL in their district. Whittier College students learned the process themselves, so that they could work with the ELL student assigned to them, who they would then tutor throughout the semester. The Road to Reclassification process teaches ELLs to set quarterly and measureable goals for themselves that eventually lead to reclassification out of ELL status. This was a process that was both empowering and self-advocating for the ELLs themselves, but also taught Whittier College students how to mentor and advocate for each of the students that they worked with. Through this process, both ELLs and their mentors learned about their strengths and areas of needs, and the mentors were able to tailor their one-on-one tutoring to those specific needs. The majority of ELLs needed support with reading and writing, so Professor Soto incorporated scaffolding strategies that Whittier College students could use with their ELLs. These were also reading and writing strategies that some of Soto's students needed themselves and were able to use to complete their own writing assignments, as this was a writing-intensive course. Whittier College students then kept a reflective journal that they added to each time they worked with the ELL student assigned to them. At the end of the semester, Whittier College students wrote an essay about what they learned through the process, including highlights from their journals. The course inspired several students to become teachers and others learned to give back to their communities, as Whittier High School is down the street from Whittier College. Still others decided to continue their tutoring experience with another mentoring course offered by the Education Department. Student evaluations also suggested that the course design allowed first-year students at Whittier College to feel as if they belonged to the community and supported their own acclimation to the college.

1. What kinds of mentoring programs like the one at Whittier High School might you consider?

2. How would your students benefit from such collaborations with community partners?

3. What are the steps needed for creating meaningful culturally responsive service-learning projects?

1. What kinds of community service-learning projects might you want your students to engage in and why?

2. What concepts or themes connect to resources or partnerships in the community?

CONCLUSION

During the writing of our book, DeAndre Arnold, a senior at Barber Hill High School in Texas, was suspended from school for having hair in dreadlocks, an identity that he and his family use to express their Trinidadian cultural and historic roots (Asmelash, 2020). He tied his hair above his shirt collar thinking that he was respectful of and adhering to the school's rules. In response, school authorities suspended him for violating their grooming and hair code.

Throughout our book, we looked closely at the big picture of "what" and "who" we teach. We also looked at this from a micro lens in the moment-to-moment inter-actions and conversations we hold with students, the conversations they have with each other, and the conversations we have on their behalf. The goal of our book is to be proactive by looking for practices that support students to feel secure in knowing that they are members of their classroom and school communities, as well as valued and competent.

One of the greatest features of service-learning projects is their capacity to raise awareness and familiarity, as well as embrace our ever-changing student and family populations so that students such as DeAndre Arnold—and his family—are seen and valued for who they are and what they have to offer to all of us. There is no better time to engage in responsive schooling practices to ensure the success of all students than right now.

References

Adams, D. and Hamm, M. (2014). *Teaching Math, Science and Technology in Schools Today: Guidelines for educating both eager and reluctant learners*, 2nd edition. New York, NY: Rowman and Littlefield.

Agar, M. (2006). Culture: Can You Take It Anywhere? *International Journal of Qualitative Methods, 5*(2).

Agar, M. (1995). *Language Shock: Understanding the culture of conversation*. New York, NY: William Morrow.

Aguilar, E. (2012). Listening to students. *Edutopia*. Retrieved from http:// www.edutopia .org/blog/listening-to-students-elena-aguilar

Akom, A. A. (2003). "Re-examining resistance as oppositional behavior: The Nation of Islam and the creation of a black achievement ideology." *Sociology of Education, 76* (4), 305–325.

Allen, J., Beaty, J., Dean, A., Jones, J., Smith Mathew, S., McCreight, J., Schwedler, E. and Simmons, A.M. (2015). *Family Dialogue Journals: School home partnerships that support student learning*. New York, NY: Teachers College Press and Berkeley, CA: National Writing Project.

American Psychological Association. (2003). Guidelines on multicultural education, training, research, practice, and organizational change for psychologists. *American Psychologist, 58*, 377–402. doi:10.1037/0003- 066X.58.5.377

Anzaldúa, G. (1999). *Borderlands: La Frontera: The New Mestiza*, 2nd ed. San Francisco, CA: Aunt Lute Books.

ASCD. (2019a). The ASCD Whole Child Approach. Retrieved from: http://www.ascd.org/whole -child.aspx

ASCD (2019b). The Whole Child Initiative: healthy. Retrieved from: http://www.ascd.org /programs/The-Whole-Child/Healthy.aspx

Asmelach, L. (2020). If this Texas student doesn't cut his dreadlocks, he won't get to walk at graduation. It's another example of hair discrimination, some say. Retrieved from: https:// www.cnn.com/2020/01/23/us/barbers-hill-isd-dreadlocks-deandre-arnold-trnd/index.html

Bassey, Magnus. (2016). Culturally Responsive Teaching: Implications for Educational Justice. Education Sciences. 6. 35. 10.3390/educsci6040035.

Bailey, F. and Pransky, K. (2014). *Memory at Work in the Classroom: Strategies to help underachieving students.* Alexandria, VA: ASCD.

Beeman, K. & Urow, C. (2012). *Teaching for Biliteracy.* Philadelphia, PA: Calson Publishing.

Biswas-Dienera, R., Kashdan, T. B., & Gurpal, M. (2011). A dynamic approach to psychologicalstrength development and intervention. Journal of Positive Psychology, 6(2), 106–118.

Blair, S.N. (2009). Physical inactivity: the biggest public health problem of the 21st century. *British Journal of Sports Medicine* 43:1-2.

Blankstein, A. B. and Noguera, P. (2016). Achieving excellence through equity for every student. In Blankstein, A.B. and Noguera, P. *Excellence Through Equity: Five principles of courageous leadership to guide achievement for every student.* Alexandria, VA: ASCD.

Boykin, A. W. (1994). Afrocultural expression and its implications for schooling. In E. R. Hollins, J. E. King & W. C. Haymen (Eds.), *Teaching Diverse Populations* (pp. 243–256). Albany, NY: State University of New York Press.

Brockton High School Guidance Newsletter. Volume II. (December, 2007). *Get Involved in New Programs at BHS.* Retrieved from: https://www.bpsma.org/uploaded/Schools/Brockton High_School/Guidance/Newsletters/December_Newsletter_2007.pdf

Brockton High School Course of Study Guide. (2019–2020). Retrieved from: (https://resources.finalsite.net/images/v1553016871/brockton/jhc7sq0bn788sahl1d3s/BHSCourse ofStudyGuide19-20.pdf

Brophy, J.E. (1983). Research on the Self-Fulfilling Prophecy and Teacher Expectations. *Journal of Educational Psychology* 75: 631–661.

Burns, H., & Miller, W. (2012). The Learning Gardens Laboratory: Teaching sustainability and developing sustainable food systems through unique partnerships. *Journal of Agriculture, Food Systems, and Community Development,* 2(3), 69–78. http://dx.doi.org/10.5304/jafscd.2012.023.003.

Campbell Jones, F., Campbell Jones, B., and Lindsey, R.B. (2010). *The cultural proficiency journey: moving beyond ethical barriers toward profound school change.* Thousand Oaks, CA: Corwin Press.

Calderón, M. &.Minaya-Rowe, L. (2010). *Preventing long-term ELs: Transforming schools to meet core standards.* Thousand Oaks, CA: Corwin Press.

Center for Service-Learning and Civic Engagement Toolkit. (2015). University of Michigan.

Chen, X. (2000). Growing up in a collectivist culture: socialization and social-emotional development in Chinese children. In A.L. Comunian and U.P Gielan (Eds). International perspectives on human development (pp. 331–353). Lengerich Germany: Pabst Science Publishers.

Cohen, E.G. and Lotan, R. (2014*). Designing Groupwork: Strategies for the heterogeneous classroom* (10th edition). New York, NY: Teachers College Press.

Coleman, J. S., Campbell, E. Q., Hobson, C. J., McPartland, F., Mood, A. M., Weinfeld, F. D., et al. (1966). Equality of educational opportunity. Washington, DC: U.S. Government Printing Office.

Connors, K. & Seifer, S. (2005). Reflection in higher education service-learning. [Fact sheet] Learn and Serve America's National Service-Learning Clearinghouse.

Darling-Hammond, L. (2006). Constructing 21st-Century Teacher Education. *Journal of Teacher Education, 57*(3), 300–314. https://doi.org/10.1177/0022487105285962

Darling-Hammond, L., Austin, K., Lit, Ira, Nasir, N. with Luis Moll and Gloria Ladson Billings (n.d.). Kim Austin, Ira Lit, and Na'ilah Nasir with Contributions From Luis Moll and Gloria Ladson-Billings. *Session 6: The Classroom Mosaic: Culture and Learning*, Stanford University School of Education. Retrieved from: https://www.learner.org/courses/learningclassroom/support/06_culture.pdf

Data Resource Center for Child and Adolescent Health. (2011/2012). National Survey of Children's Health. Retrieved from http://www.childhealthdata.org/docs/drc/aces-databrief_version-1-0.pdf

DeCapua, A. & Marshall, H. (2010). Serving ELLs with limited or interrupted education: intervention that works. *TESOL Journal*, 1, 49-70. Retrieved October 31, 2013 from http://www.tesolmedia.com/docs/TJ/firstissue/06_TJ_DeCapuaMarshall.pdf

Delpit, L. (1995). *Other People's Children.* New York, NY: New Press.

Dewey, J. (1910). *How We Think.* Boston, MA: D.C. Heath and Company.

Dewey, J. (1933). *How We Think: A restatement of the relation of reflective thinking to the educative process.* New York, NY: Dover Publications.

Dewey, J. (1938). *Experience and Education.* New York, NY: Collier Books.

Di'Angelo, R. (2018). *White Fragility: Why it's so hard for white people to talk about racism.* Boston, MA: Beacon Press.

Duncan-Andrade, J. (2009). *Note to Educators: Hope required when growing roses.* Cambridge, MA: Harvard Educational Review.

Duncan-Andrade, J. (2018). Why critical hope may be the resource kids need most from their teachers. KQED news article.

Dunn, B. (2005). Confessions of an Underperforming Teacher. In S. Nieto (Ed). *Why We Teach.* New York, NY: Teachers College Press. p. 180.

Dusek, J. B. & Joseph, G. (1986). The bases of teacher expectancies: A meta-analysis. *Journal of Educational Psychology, 75*, 327–346.

Dweck, C. (2006). *Mindset: The new psychology of success.* New York: Ballantine Books.

Dweck, C., Walton, G. M., Cohen, G. L. (2014). *Academic tenacity: Mindsets and skills that promote long-term learning.* Retrieved from: https://ed.stanford.edu/sites/default/files/manual/dweck-walton-cohen-2014.pdf

Edwards, P.A., Domke. L., and White, K. (2017). Closing the parent gap in changing school districts. In Wepner, S. B. and Gomez, D. W. (Eds). *Challenges Facing Suburban Schools: promising responses to changing student populations.* Lanham, MD: Rowman & Littlefield. pp. 109-123.

Edmondson, A. C. (March 2004). Learning from Mistakes Is Easier Said Than Done: Group and organizational influences on the detection and correction of human error. *Journal of Applied Behavioral Science.* 40(1). pp. 66–90 DOI: 10.1177/0021886304263849.

Education Commission of the States (January, 2014*). High School Graduation Requirement or Credit toward Graduation—Service-Learning/Community Service.* Retrieved from: http://ecs.force.com/mbdata/mbc est3RTE?Rep=SL1301

EEOC (N.D.). Equal Employment Opportunity Commission. History, 35th anniversary. Retrieved: https://www.eeoc.gov/eeoc/history/35th/thelaw/civil_rights_act.html

Endo, R. and Wong, V. (2019). Lau v. Nichols, 1974. In L. Dong (Ed.) *25 Events That Shaped Asian American History: An Encyclopedia of the American Mosaic.* Santa Barbara, CA: Greenwood. pp. 339–347.

Enterprise News. (May 1, 2014). *Success of Programs Speaks Well of BHS.* Retrieved from: https://www.bpsma.org/uploaded/Schools/BrocktonHigh_School/Boxer_Round-Up /2013-2014/5.1.14_BoxerRoundUp.pdf

Epstein, J.L. (1986). Parents' reaction to teacher practices of parent involvement. *Elementary School Journal*, 86, 277–294.

Epstein, J. L. (1995). School, Family, and Community Partnerships: Caring for the children we share. *Phi Delta Kappan*, 76(9), 701-712.

Epstein, J. L. (2001). *School, Family, and Community Partnerships: Preparing educators and improving schools.* Boulder, CO: Westview Press.

Epstein, J. L. (2011). *School, Family, and Community Partnerships: Preparing educators and improving schools* (2nd ed.). Philadelphia, PA: Westview Press.

Epstein, J. L. (2018). *School, Family, and Community Partnerships: Preparing educators and improving schools.* Boulder, CO: Westview Press.

Epstein, J. L. and Associates. (2019). *School, Family, and Community Partnerships: Your handbook in action* (4th edition). Thousand Oaks, CA: Corwin Press.

Epstein, J. L. and Associates. (2009*). School, Family, and Community Partnerships: Your handbook in action* (3rd edition). Thousand Oaks, CA: Corwin Press.

Fang, Z. & Schleppegrell, M.J. (2010). Disciplinary literacies across content areas: Supporting reading through functional language analysis. *Journal of Adolescent & Adult Literacy,* 53, 587-597.

Ferlazzo, L. (2011). Involvement or Engagement? *Educational Leadership.* Alexandria, VA: ASCD.

Floyd, D. T., & McKenna, L. (2003). National youth organizations in the United States: Contributions to civil society. In D. Wertlieb, F. Jacobs, and R. M. Lerner (Eds.), *Handbook of applied developmental science: Promoting positive child, adolescent, and family development through research, policies, and programs* (pp. 11–26). Thousand Oaks, CA: Sage.

Freeman, Y.S. and Freeman, D.E. (2009). Academic language for English language learners and struggling readers: how to help students succeed across content areas. Portsmouth, NH: Heinemann

Freire, P. (1994). *Capitalism and under-development in Latin America.* New York, NY: Monthly Review.

Freire, P. (1998). *Pedagogy of freedom: Ethics, democracy, and civic courage.* Lanham, MD: Rowman & Littlefield.

Freire, P. (2001). *Pedagogy of the oppressed.* (M.B. Ramos, Trans.). New York, NY: Continuum. (Original work published 1970).

Fullan, M. and Hargreaves, A. (2012). *Professional Capitol: Transforming teaching in every school.* New York, NY: Teachers College Press.

Gamoran, A. and Long, D.A. (December, 2006). *Equality of Educational Opportunity: A 40-year retrospective.* Retrieved from WCER: 28.

Gauvain, M. (2001). *The Social Context of Cognitive Development.* New York, NY: Guilford Press.

Gay, Geneva. (2010). *Culturally Responsive Teaching: Theory, Research, and Practice.* 2nd ed. Multicultural Education Series. New York, New York: Teachers College Press.

Gay, G. & Kirkland, K. (2003). Developing cultural critical consciousness and self-reflection in preservice teacher education. *Theory into Practice, 42*(3), 181–187.

Gay, G. (2013). Teaching to and through cultural diversity. *Curriculum Inquiry, 43*(1), 48–70.

Gee, J. (2010). A situated sociocultural approach to literacy and technology. In E. A. Baker, *The New Literacies: Multiple Perspectives on Research and Practice.* New York, NY: Guilford Press.

Gee, J.P. (2009). A situated sociocultural approach to literacy and technology. Retrieved September 17, 2013: http://www.jamespaulgee.com/node/6

Gibbons, P. (2016). Scaffolding Language, Scaffolding Learning. Portsmouth, NH: Heinemann.

Ginsberg, K. (with Jablow, M. M.). (2015). *Building Resilience in Children and Teens* (2nd ed.). Elk Grove Village, IL: American Academy of Pediatrics.

Goldenberg, C. & Coleman, R. (2010). *Promoting academic achievement among English learners: A guide to the research.* Thousand Oaks, CA: Corwin.

González, N. (2005). Beyond Cultures: The hybridity of funds of knowledge. In N. González, L. Moll & C. Amanti, C (Eds.). *Funds of Knowledge: Theorizing practices in households, communities, and classrooms* (pp. 29-46). Mahwah, NJ: Lawrence Erlbaum.

González, N., Moll, L. C., & Amanti, C. (Eds.). (2005). *Funds of knowledge: Theorizing practices in households, communities, and classrooms.* Mahwah, NJ: Lawrence Erlbaum.

González, N., Moll, L. C. & Amanti, C. (2005). Introduction. In N. González, L. Moll & C. Amanti, C (Eds.). (2005). *Funds of Knowledge: Theorizing practices in households, communities, and classrooms* (pp. 1-28). Mahwah, NJ: Lawrence Erlbaum.

González, N., Moll, L., Tenery, M. F., Rivera, A., Rendon, P., Gonzales, R. & Amanti, C. (2005). Funds of knowledge for teaching in Latino households. In N. González, L. Moll & C. Amanti (Eds.), *Funds of Knowledge: Theorizing practices in households, communities, and classrooms* (pp. 89–118). Mahwah, NJ: Lawrence Erlbaum.

Halliday, M. A. K. (1994). *An introduction to functional grammar* (2nd ed.). London, UK: Edward Arnold.

Halliday, M. A. K. (2003). *On language and linguistics.* New York, NY: Continuum.

Hattie, J. A. (2008). *Visible learning: A synthesis of over 800 meta-analyses relating to achievement.* New York, NY: Routledge.

Henderson, A.T. and Dahm, B. (November 2013). *The Pathway From Fortress School to Partnership School.* Educational Leadership. Retrieved from: https://www.edweek.org/ew/section/infographics/the-pathway-to-a-partnership-school.html?r=809761821

Henderson, A. T., Mapp, K. L., Johnson, V. R. & Davies, D. (2007). *Beyond the Bake Sale: The essential guide to family-school partnerships.* New York, NY: The New Press.

Henderson, A.T. (n.d.). Family engagement: Let's go beyond the bake sale! Louisiana State Personnel Development Grant. Retrieved from: http://www.lsna.net/uploads/lsna/documents/beyond_the_bake_sale.pdf

Hertel, R. & Johnson, M. M. (2013). How the traumatic experiences of students manifest in school settings. In E. Rossen & R. Hull (Eds.), *Supporting and Educating Traumatized Students: A guide for school-based professionals* (pp. 23-35). New York, NY: Oxford University Press.

Hofstede, G. & Hofstede, G.J. (2005). *Cultures and Organizations: Software of the mind.* New York, NY: McGraw Hill.

Hofstede, G. (2001). *Culture's Consequences. Comparing values behaviors, institutions, and organizations across nations* (2nd edition). Thousand Oaks, CA: Sage.

Hollins, E. & Guzman, M.T. (2005). Research on preparing teachers for diverse populations. In M. Cochran Smith & K. Zeichner (Eds). *Studying Teacher Education: The report of the AERA panel on research and teacher education* (pp. 477-548). Mahwah, NJ: Lawrence Erlbaum.

Houston, P. T. (2011). Raising the village by bringing schools and communities together. In P.D. Houston, A.M. Blankstein, and R. W. Cole (Eds). (2010). *Leadership for Family and Community Involvement.* Thousand Oaks, CA: Corwin Press.

Hyerle, D., Curtis, S., & Alpert, L. (Eds.). (2004). *Student successes with Thinking Maps: School-based research, results, and models for achievement using visual tools.* Thousand Oaks, CA: Corwin.

IEL (2015). Institute for Educational Leadership. 2015 Award for Excellence Winner. Retrieved from: https://www.aft.org/sites/default/files/wolfe2015awardee_baltimore.pdf

Kanagala, V., Rendón, L., and Nora, A. (Winter, 2016). *A Framework for Understanding Latino/a Cultural Wealth.* Washington, DC: Diversity and Democracy.

Kolb, D.A. (1984). *Experiential Learning: Experience as the source of learning and development.* Englewood Cliffs, NJ: Prentice-Hall.

Labov, W. (2006, March). Unendangered dialects, endangered people. Paper presented at the meeting of the Georgetown University Round Table on Languages and Linguistics (GURT), Washington, DC. Retrieved from www.ling.upenn.edu/~wlabov/Papers/UDEP.pdf

Ladson-Billings, G. (1994). *The Dreamkeepers: Successful teachers of African American children.* San Francisco, CA: Jossey Bass.

Ladson-Billings, G. (1995). But that's just good teaching. *Theory into Practice, Volume 34, No. 3, pp. 159–165, Culturally Responsive Teaching.* Taylor and Francis Group.

Lawrence-Lightfoot, S. (2003). *The Essential Conversation: what parents and teachers can learn from each other.* New York, NY: Random House.

Lerner, R. M., Almerigi, J. B., Theokas, C., & Lerner, J. V. (2005). Positive youth development: A view of the issues. *Journal of Early Adolescence, 25*(1), 10–16.

Lesaux, F.D. and August, D.M. (2006). Langauge of instruction. In D. August & T. Shanahan (Eds). *Developing Literacy in Second-language Learners: Report of the National Literacy Panel on Language Minority Children and Youth.* (pp. 365–413). Mahwah, NJ: Lawrence Erlbaum.

Lesaux, N., Koda, K., Siegel, L. and Shanahan, T. (2006). Development of literacy. In D.

August & T. Shanahan (Eds). *Developing Literacy in Second-language Learners: A report of the National Literacy Panel on Language Minority Children and Youth.* (pp. 55–122). Mahwah, NJ: Lawrence Erlbaum Associates, Inc.

Lindsey, R.B., Nuri-Robins, K., Terrell, R.D, and Lindsey, D.B. (2018). Cultural Proficiency: A manual for school leaders, 4th edition. Thousand Oaks, CA: Corwin Press.

Lotan, R. (2006). Teaching teachers to build equitable classrooms. *Theory into Practice,* 45(1), 32–39.

Lotan, R. (March 2003). Group-Worthy Tasks In Creating Caring Schools. *Educational Leadership.* 60(6). pp. 72–75.

Love, N., Stiles, K. E., Mundry, S., & DiRanna, K. (2008). *The data coach's guide to improving learning for all students: Unleashing the power of collaborative inquiry.* Thousand Oaks, CA: Corwin Press.

Luke, Allan. (2000). Critical literacy in Australia: A matter of context and standpoint. *Journal of Adolescent & Adult Literacy. 43.*

Lyle, J. (1994). *Regenerative design for sustainable development.* New York, NY: Wiley Press.Mapp, K. L. (2014). Building capacity for effective family school partnerships: Retrieved from: https://face.madison.k12.wi.us/files/face/Building-the-Capacity-for-Effective-Family-School-Partnerships.pptx

Maslow, A. H. (1987). *Motivation and Personality (3rd ed.).* Delhi, India: Pearson Education.

Maslow, A. H. (1999). *Toward a Psychology of Being* (3rd ed.). New York, NY: John Wiley & Sons.

Massachusetts Curriculum Frameworks. (2017). *English Language Arts and Literacy.* Grades Pre-Kindergarten to 12, page 150. Retrieved from: http://www.doe.mass.edu/frameworks/ela/2017-06.pdf

Menjívar, C. & Cervantes, A. G. (November, 2016). The effects of parental undocumented status on families and children. Retrieved from http://www.apa.org/pi/families/resources/newsletter/2016/11/undocumented-status.aspx

Mehan, H., Villanueva, I., Hubbard, L. & Lintz, A. (1996). *Constructing School Success: The consequences of untracking low-achieving students.* Cambridge, UK: Cambridge University Press.

The Metropolitan Center for Research on Equity and Transformation of Schools. (2019). *Culturally Responsive Curriculum Scorecard:* NYU Steinhardt. Retrieved from: https://steinhardt.nyu.edu/metrocenter/resources/culturally-responsive-scorecard

Mitchell, T.D. (2007). *Critical Service-Learning as Social Justice Education: A Case study of the Citizen Scholars Program, Equity & Excellence in Education,* 40:2, 101–112, DOI: 10.1080/10665680701228797

Moll, L. C., Amanti, C., Neff, D. & González, N. (1992). Funds of knowledge for teaching: Using a qualitative approach to connect homes and classrooms. *Theory into Practice,* 31, 132–141. Moll, L. C. (2015). Foreword. In J. Allen, J. Beaty, A. Dean, J. Jones, S. Smith, Mathew, J. McCreight, . . . & A. M. Simmons, (Eds.), Family dialogue journals: School home partner-ships that support student learning (p. vii). New York: Teachers College Press.

Moon, J. (1999). Reflection in learning and professional development. London : Kogan Page Limited, Stylus Publishing, Inc.

Morris, C. G. & Maisto, A. A. (2002). *Psychology: An introduction* (11th ed.). New York, NY: Pearson Education.

Morrison, K. A., Robbins, H. H. & Rose, D. G. (2008). Operationalizing culturally relevant pedagogy: a synthesis of classroom-based research. *Equity and Excellence in Education Journal:* Routledge.

National Academies of Sciences, Engineering, and Medicine. (2017). *Promoting the educational success of children and youth learning English: Promising futures.* Washington, DC: The National Academies Press. DOI:10.17226/24677

National Center for Education Statistics. Public high school 4-year adjusted cohort graduation. https://nces.ed.gov/ccd/tables/ACGR_RE_and_characteristics_2016-17.asp

National Center for Education Statistics (May, 2018). *Characteristics of Postsecondary Faculty: The condition of education.* Retrieved December 21, 2018: https://nces.ed.gov/programs/coe/indicator_csc.asp

National Park Service. (n.d.). Civil Rights Act of 1964. Retrieved from: NPS.org

Nieto, S. (2014). Introduction from why we teach to why we teach now. In S. Nieto (Ed.) *Why We Teach Now.* New York, NY: Teachers College Press.

Noguera, P. (2002). Joaquin's Dilemma. *In Motion* magazine. Retrieved from: http://www.inmotionmagazine.com/er/pnjoaq1.html

Ogbu, J. (1985). Cultural-ecological influences on minority education. *Language Arts*, vol. 62(8).860–869.Ogbu, J. U. (1999). Beyond Language: Ebonics, Proper English, and Identity in a Black-American Speech Community. *American Educational Research Journal*, 36(2), 147–184.

Oluo, I. (2017). So You Want to Talk About Race. New York, NY: Hatchette Book Group, Inc.

Park, V., Groth, C., Bradley, J., and Rorrer, A. (2018). Reclaiming turnaround for equity and excellence: Leadership moves to build capacity for teaching and learning. In Meyers, C.V. and Darwin, M.J. (Eds). *International Perspectives on Leading Low-Performing Schools.* Charlotte, NC: Information Age Publishing. pp. 11–34.

Pedro Pires Institute for Cape Verdean Studies. (N.D.). Retrieved from: https://microsites.bridgew.edu/capeverdeanstudiesPelkey, L. (2001). In the LD bubble. In P. Rodis, M.L. Boscardin, and A. Garrod (Eds.) *Learning Disabilities and Life Stores.* (pp. 17-28). White Plains, NY: Pearson.

Peregoy, S.E. & Boyle, O.F. (2008). *Reading, writing and learning in ESL: A resource book for teaching K–12 English learners,* 5th ed.). New York, NY: Pearson.

Peregoy, S.E. & Boyle, O.F. (2017). *Reading, writing and learning in ESL: A resource book for teaching K-12 English learners,* seventh ed.). New York, NY: Pearson.

Pickeral, T., Lennon, T., Piscatelli, J. (2008). *Service-learning Policies and Practices: A research-based advocacy paper.* Denver, CO: National Center for Learning and Citizenship.

Pierce, C. M. (1970). Offensive Mechanisms. In F. B. Barbour (Ed.), *The Black Seventies* (pp. 265–282). Boston, MA: Porter Sargent Publisher.

Pransky, K. (2008). *Beneath the Surface: The hidden realities of teaching culturally and linguistically diverse young learners K-6.* Portsmouth, NH: Heinemann.

Pransky, K. and Bailey, F. (Dec.-Jan. 2003). To meet your students where they are, first you have to find them: Working with culturally and linguistically diverse at-risk students. *Reading Teacher.* 56(4). pp. 370-383.

Quezada, M. (2016). Strengthening relationships with families in the school community: Can school leaders make a difference? *Voices in Urban Education, 44,* 23–31.

Ramirez, J. D. (2010). "Building Family Support for Student Achievement: CABE Project INSPIRE Parent Leadership Development Program," *The Multilingual Educator* (March).

Richards, J. C. (2015). *Key Issues in Language Teaching.* Cambridge University Press. Cambridge, United Kingdom.

RMC Research Corporation. (2009). *K-12 Service-Learning Project Planning Toolkit.* Scotts Valley, CA: National Service-Learning Clearinghouse. Retrieved from: https://community.ksde.org/LinkClick.aspx?fileticket=kbpBbLMvts8%3D&tabid=4473

Rogoff, B. (2003). *The Cultural Nature of Human Development.* New York, NY: Oxford University Press.

Rogoff, B. (2009). *The Cultural Nature of Human Development.* New York, NY: Oxford University Press.

Rogoff, B. (1990). *Apprenticeship in Thinking: Cognitive development in social context.* New York, NY: Oxford University Press.

Rothstein-Fisch, C. and Trumbull, E. (2008). Managing diverse classrooms: How to build on students' cultural strengths. Alexandria, VA: ASCD.

Ryan, M. (2012). *Service learning after Learn and Serve America: How five states are moving forward.* Denver, CO: Education Commission of the States. Retrieved from http://www.ecs.org/clearinghouse/01/02/87/10287.pdf

Santa Clara County Office of Education in California (2016). My Name, My Identity: Declaration of Self. Retrieved from: https://www.mynamemyidentity.org/

Schwartz, K. (2018). Why Critical Hope May Be the Resource Kids Need Most From Their Teachers. *MindShift.*

Schwartz, S. (2019). Next step in diversity training: Teachers learn to face their unconscious dias. Bethesda, MD: Education Week.

Seligman, M. E. P., Rashid, T., & Parks, A. C. (2006). Positive psychotherapy. *American Psychologist, 61*(8), 774–788.

Soto, I. (2012). *ELL Shadowing as a Catalyst for Change.* Thousand Oaks, CA: Corwin Press.

Soto, I. (2016). *Academic English Mastery Series.* Thousand Oaks, CA: Corwin Press.Soto, I., Besocke, K. & Magana, D. (2015). Creating Classroom Buzz. Topanga, CA: Language Magazine.

Soto, I. and Hetzel, J. (2009). *The Literacy Gaps: Bridge-building strategies for English language learners and standard English learners.* Thousand Oaks, CA: Corwin Press.

Southern Education Foundation. (2015). A new majority: Low income students now a majority in the nation's public schools [Research bulletin]. Retrieved Novem-

ber 20, 2018 from http:// www.southerneducation.org/Our-Strate gies/Research
-and-Publications/New-Maj ority-Diverse-Majority-Report-Series/ANew-Majority
-2015-Update-Low-IncomeStudents-Now

Steele, C. M. (2011). *Whistling Vivaldi and other clues to how stereotypes affect us.* New
York, NY: Norton.

Steele, C. M. & Aronson, J. (1995). Stereotype threat and the intellectual test performance of
African-Americans. *Journal of Personality and Social Psychology, 69,* 797811.

Teel, K. M. and Obidah, J. E. (2008). *Building Racial and Cultural Competence in the Classroom: Strategies from urban educators.* New York, NY: Teachers College Press.

Tyler, K.M., Uqdah, A.L., Dillihunt, M.L., Beatty-Hazelbaker, R., Conner, T., Gadson, N.C.,
Henchy, A.M., Hughes, T., Mulder, S., Owens, E., Roan-Belle, C., Smith, L., & Stevens,
R. (2008). Cultural discontinuity: Towards the empirical inquiry of a major hypothesis
in education. Educational Researcher, 37, 280-297

United States Courts of Behalf of Federal Judiciary (n.d.). History: Brown v. Board of Education Re-enactment. Retrieved from: https://www.uscourts.gov/educational-resources
/educational-activities/history-brown-v-board-education-re-enactment

University of Washington. (2012). Service learning. Retrieved from: https://www.washington
.edu/teaching/topics/engaging-students-in-learning/service-learning/

U.S. Department of Education, Title IX General Provision 9101 (25). (N.D.). Retrieved from:
https://www2.ed.gov/policy/elsec/leg/esea02/pg107.html

U.S. Department of Education. (2016). *The state of racial diversity in the educator workforce.*
Retrieved from https://www2.ed.gov/rschstat/eval/highered/racial-diversity/state-racial
-diversity-workforce.pdf

U.S. Department of State. (2015). Cumulative summary of refugee admissions. Retrieved
from https://2009-2017.state.gov/j/prm/releases/statistics/251288.htm

Valenzuela, A. (1999). *Subtractive Schooling: U.S.-Mexican youth and the politics of caring.*
Albany, NY: State University of New York Press.

Vargas, C. (2019). Dr. Clemencia Vargas Interview Transcript. Retrieved from: https://www
.colorincolorado.org/dr-clemencia-vargas

Vargas, R. (Winter, 1987). Transformative knowledge. Langely, WA: In *Context Magazine.*

Vargas, R. (2008). *Family Activism: Empowering your community, beginning with family
and friends.* San Francisco, CA: Berrett-Koehler Publishers, Inc.

Vogel, L.R., (2011). Enacting social justice: Perceptions of educational leaders. *Administrative
Issues Journal: Education, Practice, and Research, 1(2),* 69-82.

Vygotsky, L. (1978). *Mind in Society* (M. Cole, Trans.). Cambridge, MA: Harvard University
Press.

WETA Public Broadcasting. (2019). The Secret of a Successful Partnership. Retrieved from:
https://youtu.be/3vke0dHWD4M?list=PLoU659hwTdDZ8acTkQ5JblfIiAgtQhuCi

White, E.B. (2006). *Charlotte's Web.* New York, NY: HarperCollins.

Wiebler, L. R. (2013). Developmental differences in response to trauma. In E. Rossen & R.
Hull (Eds.), *Supporting and educating traumatized students: A guide for school-based
professionals* (pp. 39–47). New York, NY: Oxford University Press.

Wikipedia. (2019). Thinking Maps. Retrieved from: https://en.wikipedia.org/wiki/Thinking _Maps

Wolfe Street Academy (2019a). Wolfe Street Academy: An overview. Colorín Colorado. Retrieved from: https://www.colorincolorado.org/video/wolfe-street-academy (1)

Wolfe Street Academy (2019b). ELL population at Wolfe Street Academy. Colorín Colorado. Retrieved from: https://www.colorincolorado.org/video/wolfe-street-academy (2)

Wolfe Street Academy (2019c). Upper Fells Point Improvement Association. Retrieved from: https://www.colorincolorado.org/video/wolfe-street-academy (3)

Wolpert-Gawron, H. (2016). What the heck is service learning? San Rafael, CA: Edutopia.

Wolpert-Gawron, H. (2019). Infographic on collaboration. Marin County, CA: Edutopia.

Yoshikawa, H. (2011). *Immigrants raising citizens: Undocumented parents and their young children*. New York, NY: Russell Sage Foundation.

Yosso, T. J. (2005) Whose culture has capital? A critical race theory discussion of community cultural wealth, Race Ethnicity and Education, 8:1, 69-91, DOI: 10.1080/1361332052000341006

Zacarian, D., Alvarez-Ortiz, L., Haynes, J. (2017). Teaching to Strengths: supporting students living with trauma, violence and chronic stress. Alexandria, VA: ASCD.

Zacarian, D. and Dove, M. (2019). From nobody cares to every community cares. In *Breaking Down the Wall*. Thousand Oaks, CA: Corwin Press.

Zacarian, D. and Silverstone, M.A. (2020). *Raising Students' Voices in Diverse Classroom Settings*. Alexandria, VA: ASCD.

Zacarian, D. and Silverstone, M.A. (2015). *In It Together: How student, family, and community partnerships advance engagement and achievement in diverse classrooms*. Thousand Oaks, Corwin Press.

Zacarian, D. (2015). *Mastering Academic Language: A framework for supporting student achievement*. Thousand Oaks, VA: Corwin Press.

Zacarian, D. & Haynes, J. (2012). *The Essential Guide for Teaching Beginning English Learners*. Thousand Oaks, CA: Corwin Press.

Zacarian, D. (2011). *Transforming Schools for English Learners: A comprehensive framework for school leaders*. Thousand Oaks, CA: Corwin Press.

Zeichner, K. (2012). *Two Visions of Teaching and Teacher Education for the Twenty-first Century*. Dartmouth, MA: University of Massachusetts Dartmouth Center for Policy Analysis.

Zwiers, J. (2012). *Talk is priceless: Building students' skills for powerful academic conversations*. Paper presented at the annual conference of the Massachusetts Teachers of Speakers of Other Languages, Framingham, MA.

Index

About the Authors

Debbie Zacarian, Ed.D., is known for her expertise in strengths-based leadership, instructional, and family partnership practices with culturally and linguistically diverse student and family populations. Zacarian provides professional development, strategic planning, and policy work with school districts as well as state, national, and international agencies and organizations. Before founding Zacarian and Associates, she served on the faculty of University of Massachusetts–Amherst. Zacarian also served as an educational service agency program director in Massachusetts and led professional growth initiatives for thousands of educators, wrote English learner policies, and was the expert consultant for many school districts and state agencies. Additionally, she directed the Amherst Public Schools' English Learner program where she received state recognition.

Ivannia Soto, Ph.D., is Professor of Education at Whittier College, where she specializes in second language acquisition, systemic reform for English language learners (ELLs), and urban education. As a consultant, Soto has worked with Stanford University's School Redesign Network (SRN), WestEd, and CABE, as well as a variety of districts and county offices in California, providing technical assistance for systemic reform for ELLs and Title III. Soto is Executive Director of the Institute for Culturally and Linguistically Responsive Teaching (ICLRT) at Whittier College, whose mission it is to promote relevant research and develop academic resources for ELLs and Standard English Learners (SELs) via linguistically and culturally responsive teaching practices.